Discovering
CHRISTIAN NAMES

S. M. Jarvis

Shire Publications Ltd.

CONTENTS

Cover design by Ron Shaddock.

Copyright © 1973 and 1979 by S. M. Jarvis. First published 1973. Second edition 1979; reprinted 1983, 1986 and 1989. Number 156 in the Discovering series. ISBN 0 85263 448 X.

Printed in Great Britain by C. I. Thomas & Sons (Haverfordwest) Ltd, Press Buildings, Merlins Bridge, Haverfordwest, Dyfed.

PREFACE

In the distillation of the essence of a book like this a vast flow of information must be read and understood before the author adds his own original research. So I am a wiser man than I was eighteen months ago—and my thanks to other compilers are expressed in the form of a list of books for further reference. What I learned from them, and from half a lifetime as a librarian, was the true nature of the study of 'onomastics'—the science of personal and place names. Such a study must begin in the cradle of civilisation when names were first given because many of those names have persisted throughout history to be used commonly today.

Semitic names, of which the majority are the Hebrew names perpetuated in the Bible, were not invented words, but constituted a message based on the conjunction of two elements. Thus, Jacob means 'taking by the heel' because that was the manner of his birth. In a small community it was possible to give every individual just such a separate name, but with large families and increasing tribes this could not be continued, so children were often named in honour of earlier people, particularly of tribal leaders, folk heroes and their families.

However, a growing number of people needed to be identified from the limited stock of names, so 'patronymics' developed and are detectable in surnames surviving round the world today from Scandinavia with names like 'Peterson' to the Middle East—'Simon bar Jonas' (Simon son of Jonah).

The ancient Greeks had a separate system, using the name of the father to identify the son in a simple use of the genitive form, or in the addition of a suitable element before or after the name. The father chose his children's names and would alter them as he chose. Women's names were all tied to their menfolk's, with feminine endings. But even then nicknames were common. Plato, the great philosopher who lived around 400 B.C., was named Aristocles, but his gymnastics master nicknamed him 'broad' *(platon)* and the name stuck.

The system of the Romans was much more complicated. Their highly organised society brought a three-name system into use. The *praenomen* or personal name, the *nomen* or family name, and the *cognomen* which began life as a nickname, like Caesar—'the hairy one'—and thence became the name of the branch of the original family. The Celtic and

Teutonic races had a simple but effective system based on a common stock of words considered suitable for name-making from which a combination of two such words was chosen. It is from this source that Anglo-Saxon names derived to make up a large part of our national heritage of names.

In the early days a boy was given a name at puberty—the time of initiation or circumcision. The custom of Christian baptism is linked with this as a natural development from the old religion to the new, which brought into western countries the large stock of names held in the Bible. So, in our country forenames became very diverse.

It will be obvious that forenames were first names in both senses of the word. They identified an individual absolutely in the days when every person in the settlement had their very own name. Then, when two names became necessary in western civilisation the forename took up its position in front of the family name to preserve the specific classification of the person. In modern times the desire to identify closely an individual in a rapidly increasing population has led to the invention or adaptation of names on which the Victorian parson would have looked with the gravest doubts. The flower names of those days were something of an innovation, but the advent of films in the twentieth century brought the necessity to give 'stars' names which were different and memorable and this caused a rush of invented names which television perpetuates.

MEANINGS OF NAMES

AARON—m 'Light' (Hebrew). First High Priest of the Israelites.

ABDIEL—m 'Servant of God' (Hebrew).

ABEL—m 'Son' (Hebrew). Second son of Adam, slain by his brother Cain. Abel Magwitch, character in Dickens's *Great Expectations*.

ABIAH—m 'My father is the Lord' (Hebrew).

ABIEL—m Alternative of Abiah.

ABIGAIL—f 'Father's joy' (Hebrew). Wife of David, King of Israel.

ABIUD—m 'Father in glory' (Hebrew).

ABNER—m 'Father of light' (Hebrew). Commander of Saul's army, but more recently popularised by the American 'Li'l Abner' strip cartoons.

ABRAHAM—m 'Father of a multitude' (Hebrew). Traditional progenitor of the Hebrew people. Abraham Lincoln (1809-1865)—sixteenth President of the USA.

ABSALOM—m 'Peace of the father' (Hebrew). Third son of David, King of Israel. The young clerk in Chaucer's 'Miller's Tale'.

ACHILLES—m Its original Greek meaning is obscure. Great warrior of the Trojan wars as told in Greek legend.

ACIMA—f 'The Lord will judge' (Hebrew).

ADA—f Probably shortened form of Adela. Byron's daughter (born 1815).

ADAH—f 'An ornament' (Hebrew). One of the wives of Esau. The wife of Cain. Adah Mencken—late nineteenth-century American actress and poet.

ADAIR—m 'Ford by the oak' (Celtic).

ADAM—m 'Red earth' (Hebrew). The first man, as written in the book of Genesis. Adam Smith wrote *The Wealth of Nations* (1776). *Adam Bede* by George Eliot (1859).

ADELA—f 'Noble' (Teutonic). Fourth daughter of William the Conqueror, mother of King Stephen.

ADELAIDE—f 'Nobility' (Teutonic). The popular queen of William IV from 1830 made it fashionable. Capital of South Australia, founded 1836, named after her.

ADELE—f French form of Adela.

ADELGAR—m 'Noble spear' (Teutonic).

ADELINE—f 'Noble' (Teutonic). Variant of Adela even from Norman times. Adelina Patti, born 1843, great soprano. 'Sweet Adeline'—song popular before First World War.

5

ADELPHO—m 'Brother' (Greek).

ADOLF, ADOLPH—m 'Noble wolf' (Teutonic). Also as Adolphus. Less popular since it was Hitler's forename.

ADRIAN—m 'Of the Adriatic' (Latin). From Hadrian, the Roman emperor responsible for Hadrian's Wall. But may have been prompted through Pope Adrian IV, the name adopted by Nicholas Brakespeare (died 1159), the only Englishman to become pope.

ADRIANA—f Form of Adrian. A character in Shakespeare's *Comedy of Errors*.

ADRIENNE—f French, and more popular form of Adriana.

AENEAS—m 'The chosen one' (Old Irish). The name of the son of Anchises and Aphrodite in classical legend, later used by Irish and Scots as a rendering of the root of Angus.

AERONA—f 'Berry' (Welsh).

AGATHA—f 'Good woman' (Greek). St. Agatha was a third-century martyr.

AGLAIA—f 'Beauty' (Greek). One of the three Graces in Greek mythology.

AGNES—f 'Pure' (Greek). St. Agnes, child martyr of the third century. 'From the twelfth to the sixteenth century Agnes was one of the commonest English f. names'—Withycombe. Victorian popularity helped by Keats's 'Eve of St. Agnes' (1819) and Tennyson's 'St. Agnes' Eve' (1842).

AIDAN—m 'Little fire' (Old Irish). Irish monk (died 651), founder of the church in Northumbria.

AILEEN—f Form of Eileen more common in Ireland.

AINE—f Form of Aidan which is also spelt Aithne.

AJAX—m 'Of the earth' (Greek).

ALAN—m 'Harmony' (Celtic). Norman introduction.

ALANA—f 'My child' (Irish).

ALARD—m 'Noble and strong' (Teutonic). The original Adalhard also gives rise to Adlard.

ALARIC—m 'Ruler over all' (Teutonic). King of the Visigoths (born A.D. 370) and conqueror of Rome.

ALASTAIR—m Scottish form of Alexander.

ALASTOR—m 'Avenger' (Greek).

ALBAN—m 'Of Alba' (Latin). St. Alban, first British martyr, gave his name to St. Albans.

ALBERGA—m 'Noble' (Teutonic).

ALBERIC—m 'Wise ruler' (Teutonic). Reintroduced by Normans in the form of Aubrey.

ALBERT—m 'Nobly bright' (Teutonic). Prince Albert (1819-1861) married Queen Victoria in 1840.

ALBERTA—f Form of the popular Victorian male name, but could also be named after the Canadian province.

ALBERTINE—f French diminutive of Alberta. Character in Proust's *Remembrance of Things Past* (1932).

ALBINUS—m 'White' (Latin). Usually known as Alcuin. English prelate and scholar born 735.

ALBREDA—m 'Wise council' (Teutonic).

ALCINA—f 'Maid from the sea' (Greek).

ALDA—f 'Old' (Teutonic). Sister of Oliver and wife of Orlando in the Charlemagne romances.

ALDEN—m 'Old friend' (Old English).

ALDHELM—m 'Great helmet' (Old English). Probably signifying warrior. St. Aldhelm, abbot of Malmesbury, born about 640. St. Aldhelm's Head on the Dorset coast is corrupted to St. Alban's Head.

ALDITH—f 'Great warrior' (Teutonic).

ALDOUS—m 'Old' (Teutonic). A variant of Alda. Largely confined to East Anglia. Aldous Huxley (1894-1963). English man of letters, author of *Brave New World* (1932) and many other important works.

ALDRED—m 'Great counsel' (Old English). The Archbishop of York who crowned William the Conqueror in 1066.

ALDWIN—m 'Great friend' (Old English). Gave rise to surnames Aldin, Alden, etc.

ALEC—m Short form of Alexander.

ALETHEA—f 'Truth' (Greek). Alethea Bigge was Jane Austen's friend. Charles I, when Prince of Wales, went to Spain to make the acquaintance of Princess Maria Aletea. In Ireland, Letty is a diminutive of this name.

ALEX—m Short form of Alexander.

ALEXANDER—m 'Helper of men' (Greek). Alexander the Great, born 356 B.C., conqueror of the civilised world. Eight popes have chosen this name.

ALEXANDRA—f Form of Alexander. Queen of Edward VII.

ALEXIS—m or f 'Helper' (Greek). Greek dramatist of fourth century B.C. Alexis Paul (1847-1901) French playwright and novelist, lifelong friend of Emil Zola. Much used as a male name in Russia, but in this century becoming popular for girls in Britain.

ALFONSO—m 'Eager for battle' (Teutonic). In this form the name of many kings of Spain; the last one, Alfonso XIII, was deposed in 1931 when the country became a republic.

ALFRED—m 'Wise counsellor' (Old English). Alfred the

7

Great (849-899), king of England. Alfred, Lord Tennyson, poet laureate 1850-1892.

ALFREDA—f Form of Alfred.

ALGAR—m 'Cunning spear' (Old English). Gives rise to surnames like that of Sir Edward Elgar (1857-1934), English composer.

ALGERNON—m 'The whiskered one' (Norman-French). The nickname of William de Percy, founder of the great Percy family, later Earls and Dukes of Northumberland, at the time of William the Conqueror, when most courtiers were clean-shaven.

ALICE—f 'Truth' (Greek). Probably influenced in its nineteenth-century revival by Lewis Carroll's *Alice in Wonderland* (1865), named after one of his young friends, Alice Liddell.

ALINE—f A contraction of Adeline.

ALISON—f Scottish diminutive of Alice already popular by the fourteenth century.

ALLEGRA—f 'Cheerful' (Latin).

ALMA—f 'All good' (Celtic). Its rise in Victorian times was due to the celebrated battle of Alma, in the Crimea (1854). Name of the Queen of Body Castle in Spenser's *Faerie Queene*.

ALMERIA—f From the province of south-east Spain. The character in Congreve's *The Mourning Bride* who utters the well-known line, 'Music hath charms to soothe a savage breast'.

ALMERIC—m 'Work-ruler' (Teutonic). Produced Amery and many other surnames.

ALOYSIUS—m Same as Louis. St. Aloysius died 1591 aged 23, and because of the purity of his life was declared patron saint of youth.

ALPHONSO—m Alternative spelling of Alfonso.

ALSTON—m 'Rock of nobility' (Old English).

ALTHEA—f 'Wholesome' (Greek). Immortalised in the famous poem 'To Althea from Prison' by Richard Lovelace (1618-1658).

ALVIN—m Form of Alwyn.

ALVINA—f 'White' (Spanish).

ALWYN—m 'Dear friend' (Teutonic).

AMABEL—f 'Lovable' (Latin). Sometimes spelt Amiable.

AMADEA—f Form of Amadeus.

AMADEUS—m 'Loving God' (Latin). Amadeus V (died 1323), Count of Savoy and ancestor of all the kings of Italy. Wolfgang Amadeus Mozart (1755-1791).

AMADIS—m Form of Amadeus.

AMANDA—f 'Lovable' (Latin). Apparently first appears as a character in Colley Cibber's *Love's Last Shift* (1694) and its sequel *The Relapse* by Sir John Vanbrugh.

AMARYLLIS—f 'Refreshing stream' (Greek). Developed through Latin poets to use by English poets like Spenser and Milton.

AMBER—f A modern 'precious stone' name.

AMBROSE—m 'Numbered with the immortals' (Greek). St. Ambrose was bishop of Milan in the fourth century, 'one of the most illustrious lives recorded in Church history'. Emrys is the Welsh form. 'Namby-Pamby' nickname given to Ambrose Philips, eighteenth-century poet, by his rival Henry Carey.

AMBROSINE—f Form of Ambrose. Modern French import.

AMELIA—f 'Worker' (Teutonic). In England more often represented by Emily. Princess Amelia, youngest daughter of George III, was called Emily in everyday life. Henry Fielding wrote *Amelia* in 1751.

AMERY—m Form of Amory.

AMICE—f 'Beloved' (Latin). Very popular in medieval times, but has lost ground to Amy.

AMITY—f A post-Reformation 'abstract quality' name.

AMORY—m 'Work ruler' (Teutonic). See Almeric.

AMOS—m 'Carried' (Hebrew). An Old Testament prophet.

AMUND—m 'Divine protection' (Scandinavian).

AMY—f 'A woman beloved' (Latin). Amy Robsart married Robert Dudley, Earl of Leicester, in 1550 but died mysteriously during his suit for the hand of Elizabeth I.

AMYAS—m 'Loving God' (Latin). Form of Amadeus. Amyas Leigh, hero of Kingsley's *Westward Ho!*

ANASTASIA—f 'Who shall rise again' (Greek). Often used for girls born at Easter time. The daughter of the last tsar of Russia, reputed to have survived the assassination of the entire family in 1918 during the Russian revolution.

ANATOLE—m 'Like the rising sun' (Greek).

ANCEL—m 'God-like' (Teutonic). Favourite name among the Normans.

ANDREA—f Form of Andrew, but used also for men, as Andrea del Sarto (1486-1531), Florentine painter.

ANDREANA—f Form of Andrew.

ANDREW—m 'Manly' (Greek). First disciple called by Jesus. Martyred on the X-shaped cross which is his symbol as the patron saint of Scotland.

ANDROCLES—m 'Man in his glory' (Greek).

ANGEL—m 'Messenger' (Greek). Tess's husband in Hardy's *Tess of the D'Urbervilles*. Common in Italy as Angelo.

ANGELA—f Form of Angel. Late nineteenth-century popularity, originally used for girls born about 29th September, the feast of St. Michael and All Angels.

ANGELICA—f 'Like an angel' (Latin). Painter Angelica Kauffmann was first female member of the Royal Academy (1769).

ANGUS—m 'Virtuous' (Gaelic). A thane of Scotland in Shakespeare's *Macbeth*. One of three Irish brothers who conquered Scotland and gave his name to the county and subsequently to the breed of cattle.

ANGWEN—f 'Beauteous' (Welsh).

ANITA—f Diminutive of Ann.

ANKETIL—m 'Holy fire' (Norse).

ANN(E)—f 'Grace' (Hebrew). English form of Hannah. St. Anne or Anna was the traditional mother of the Virgin Mary. Six English queens have borne the name.

ANNABEL(LA)—f 'Joy' (Gaelic). Traced back to twelfth century in Scotland, but not used elsewhere until modern times. The poem 'Annabel Lee' by Edgar Allan Poe (1849) may have spread its use.

ANNIS—f Form of Agnes.

ANNO—m Form of Arnold.

ANNONA—f 'Harvest' (Latin).

ANNORA—f 'Grace' (Hebrew).

ANSELM—m 'Holy helmeted' (Teutonic). St. Anselm (1033-1109), archbishop of Canterbury.

ANSTEY—m 'Resurrection' (Greek).

ANTHEA—f 'Like a flower' (Greek). Robert Herrick (1591-1674) wrote the poem 'To Anthea, who may command him anything'.

ANTHONY—m 'Inestimable' (Latin). Often without the H. Name of the great Roman family which included Mark Antony. St. Antony, patron saint of swineherds, established first monastery in Christian history (c 300 A.D.).

ANTIGONE—f 'Contrary birth' (Greek). Tragic daughter of Oedipus in Greek legend.

ANTONIA, ANTOINETTE—f Italian and French diminutives of Anthony. Marie Antoinette, queen of Louis XVI, was guillotined in 1793.

ANWYL—m 'Dear' (Welsh).

APHRA—f 'Dust' (Hebrew). All due to a Bible translator's error in the book of Micah. The word for dust was translated as a person's name. Aphra Behn (1640-1689), English dramatist and novelist.

APHRODITE—f 'Foam-born' (Greek). The Grecian Venus.

APRIL—f Example of the modern fashion of calling a child by the name of the month in which it was born.

AQUILA—m 'Eagle' (Latin). In early times used equally for both sexes.

ARABEL(LA)—f 'Easy to be intreated' (Latin). Late eighteenth-century romantic name. Derivation from *orabilis* is tentative.

ARAMINTA—f Seventeenth-century invention.

ARCHER—m Modern English derivation from the surname.

ARCHIBALD—m 'Sacred leader' (Teutonic).

ARDATH—f 'Flowery meadow' (Hebrew).

ARIADNE—f 'The very holy one' (Greek). Daughter of Minos, King of Crete, in Greek mythology. An asteroid (no. 43) discovered in 1857.

ARLENE—f Short form variant of Adeline.

ARMAND—m 'Soldier' (Teutonic).

ARMINEL—m 'Lord of an army' (Teutonic). Rare, but still in use in Devon, though it also had Norfolk connections. Probably from same root as Herman.

ARNOLD—m 'Eagle-strength' (Teutonic). Came over with the Conqueror, fell almost out of use, then came back strongly, perhaps through Thomas Arnold (1795-1842), headmaster of Rugby, and his son Matthew Arnold, critic, poet and essayist. Arnold Bennett (died 1931) novelist of the 'Five Towns' series.

ARTEMISIA—f 'Vigorous' (Greek). Daughter of Zeus in Greek mythology. Artemisia was the queen who built the first mausoleum—in memory of her husband Mausolus, at Halicarnassus, about the fourth century B.C.

ARTHUR—m 'High' (Celtic). The Arthurian legend gave it currency from early times. Popularised by the successes of Arthur Wellesley, Duke of Wellington, by Tennyson's *Idylls of the King,* retelling the legend, and by the fact that Queen Victoria chose it for her youngest son.

ASA—m 'Good health' (Hebrew). King of Judah.

ASHER—m 'Happy' (Hebrew).

ASPASIA—f 'Welcome' (Greek). Mistress of Pericles (c 440 B.C.). Heroine of Beaumont and Fletcher's *The Maid's Tragedy* (1619).

ASTON—m Place-name—family name derivative. Sir Aston

11

Webb (1849-1930), President of Royal Academy and architect.

ASTRID—**f** 'Divine strength' (Teutonic). Much used by Scandinavian royalty from Canute onwards.

ATHANASIA—**f** 'Immortal' (Greek).

ATHELSTAN—**m** 'Jewel of nobility' (Old English). King of Wessex (925-940).

ATHENE—**f** Meaning unknown. Goddess worshipped at the Acropolis in Athens.

ATHERTON—**m** 'Woodland dweller' (Old English).

AUBREY—**m** 'Wise ruler' (French). Equivalent of Alberic.

AUDE—**m** French version of Alda, used in England in the twelfth century.

AUDREY—**f** 'Noble might' (Old English). From Etheldreda. At St. Etheldreda's (Audrey's) Fair in the sixteenth century, cheap necklaces were sold, giving rise to 'tawdry' as a description of cheap, garish goods.

AUGUSTA—**f** Form of Augustus. For girls born in August.

AUGUSTINE—**m** Diminutive of Augustus. St. Augustine—first archbishop of Canterbury (601). The order of Augustin or Austin Friars instituted in his name became the greatest sheep farmers in England.

AUGUSTUS—**m** 'Venerable' (Latin). Used by German princes after the Reformation in imitation of Roman emperors. Augustus Toplady, clergyman, composer of 'Rock of Ages' (c 1776).

AURELIA—**f** 'Golden' (Latin). Roman family name. Charmingly translated by an earlier writer on names as 'little pretty golden lady'.

AUSTIN—**m** Form of Augustine.

AVA—**f** Manufactured modern name, possibly for film star Ava Gardner.

AVERIL—**f** 'Wild boar battle maid' (Teutonic). Often confused with Avril, French for April.

AVICE—**f** 'War refuge' (Teutonic).

AVRIL—**f** 'April' (French). Used for girls born in this month.

AYLMER—**m** 'Far-famed' (Teutonic). Gave rise to the American form of Elmer.

AYLWIN—**m** 'Wise friend' (Old English).

AZARIAH—**m** 'Helped by God' (Hebrew).

BABETTE—**f** French diminutive of Elizabeth.

BALDRIC—**m** 'Bold ruler' (Teutonic). Baldred was an early bishop of Glasgow.

BALTHASAR—**m** 'Wise in battle' (Persian). The name given, by popular account, to one of the Three Wise Men.

No less than five Shakespeare characters.

BAMBER—m Family name used in the Gascoigne family as a forename since the eighteenth century.

BARBARA—f 'Stranger' (Greek). One of the four third-century virgin saints. 'Barbara was said to be a maiden of Heliopolis, whose Christianity was revealed by her insisting that a bath-chamber should be built with three windows instead of two, in honour of the chief mystery of the Creed. Her cruel father beheaded her with his own hands, and was immediately destroyed by thunder and lightning . . .' (C. M. Yonge).

BARCLAY—m Place-name surname derivation.

BARDOLPH—m 'Cunning wolf' (Teutonic). Falstaff's companion in three of Shakespeare's plays.

BARNABAS—m 'Consoling son' (Hebrew). St. Paul's travelling companion stoned to death as a martyr. *Barnaby Rudge* by Charles Dickens.

BARRY—m 'Looking straight at the mark'. Thackeray's *Barry Lyndon* is the story of an Irish rogue. A Welsh town and an Antarctic islet.

BARTHOLOMEW—m 'Son of Talmai'. Ancestral name of the apostle Nathaniel. St. Bartholomew's Hospital founded by Rahere, Court Jester to Henry I, who claimed to have been cured through a vision of the saint.

BASIL—m 'Kingly' (Greek). St. Basil the Great (329-379) was one of the Fathers of the early church.

BASILLA or BASILIA—f Form of Basil.

BASTIAN—m Short form of Sebastian.

BAT—m Short form of Bartholomew.

BATHSHEBA—f 'Voluptuous' (Hebrew). The wife of Uriah and later the wife of David and mother of Solomon.

BAXTER—m 'Baker' (Old English). Early surname.

BEATA—f 'Blessed' (Latin).

BEATRICE—f 'Bringer of joy' (Latin). Sometimes Beatrix as Beatrix Potter, author of the 'Peter Rabbit' children's books. Beatrice is a key character in Shakespeare's *Much Ado About Nothing*. Dante's guide through Paradise in his *Divine Comedy* was Beatrice.

BEAUREGARD—m 'Handsome' (French).

BEDELIA—f Form of Bridget.

BEDWIN—m 'As the birch tree' (Welsh).

BELINDA—f 'Sinuous' (Teutonic). Heroine of Pope's *Rape of the Lock* (1714) and title of Maria Edgeworth's novel published 1801.

BELLAMY—m 'Good friend' (French). From the surname.

BENEDICT—m 'Blessed' (Latin). Occurs also as Bennet. St. Benedict (490-542) founder of the Benedictine order. A long line of popes bore this name.

BENEDICTA—f Female form of Benedict. The Spanish form of Benita is used in the USA.

BENJAMIN—m 'Son of the right hand' (Hebrew). Youngest son of Jacob. Big Ben—named after Sir Benjamin Hall, Commissioner of Works when it was installed.

BENTLEY—m 'Meadow' (Old English). From the surname.

BERENGARIA—f 'Bear spear' (Teutonic). Queen of Richard I. Little used, but the great transatlantic liner of the name did give rise to some girls being named after it.

BERENICE—f 'Bringer of victory' (Greek). Known better in recent times in its short form of Bernice. Racine's *Bérenice*, 1670, is founded on the story of the Roman emperor Titus and the Jewish princess Berenice.

BERKELEY—m Place-name derivation.

BERNADETTE—f Diminutive of Bernard. St. Bernadette of Lourdes (1844-1879). The name was revived through the novel about her, *Song of Bernadette* by Franz Werfel (1942) and the subsequent film.

BERNARD—m 'Tough as a bear' (Teutonic). St. Bernard of Menthon (923-1008) founded the hospices which gave aid to travellers in the Alps. Patron saint of mountaineers.

BERNICE—f Short form of Berenice.

BERTHA—f 'Bright' (Old English). The mother of Charlemagne, known as 'Bertha Big-foot'. Revived in Victorian times. Big Bertha—long-range gun used by Germans to shell Paris in 1918.

BERTRAM—m 'Perky as a raven' (Teutonic).

BERTRAND—m 'Bright shield' (Teutonic). Bertrand Russell, third Earl, 'the greatest philosopher of the present century'.

BERYL—f The name of a precious stone, derived from a Greek word of unknown derivation.

BESS, BESSIE, BETSY, BETTY—f All variations of Elizabeth which have been used in their own right.

BEULAH—f 'Married' (Hebrew).

BEVERLEY—m or f Place-name derivation.

BEVIS—m 'Bow' (Teutonic). The hero of Richard Jefferies's *Bevis, the Story of a Boy* (1882).

BIANCA—f Italian form of Blanche. Appears in Shakespeare's *Othello* and *The Taming of the Shrew*.

BIDDULPH—m 'Commanding wolf' (Teutonic).

BIDDY—f Short form of Bridget.

BLAIR—m 'Plain dweller' (Gaelic).

BLANCHE—f 'White' (French). Charles Lamb wrote in 1808, 'Blanche is out of fashion'. Today the Italian form Bianca is much in currency.

BLEDDYN—m 'Little wolf' (Welsh).

BLODWEN—f 'Pale as the flower' (Welsh).

BLYTH—m 'Happy' (Old English). Blythe for a girl.

BONAMY—m 'Good friend' (French).

BONAR—m 'Courteous' (Old French).

BONIFACE—m 'Well-doer' (Latin). A third-century saint and a line of popes from 418.

BOOTH—m 'Herdsman' (Old English).

BORIS—m 'Fighter' (Russian). Kings of Bulgaria from the earliest times. Boris Goudenoff (died 1605), the tsar of Russia who proposed to our Queen Elizabeth, is the subject of plays and operas.

BOTOLF, BOTOLPH—m 'Commanding wolf' (Teutonic). St. Botolf (died 680) is claimed to have introduced the Benedictine rule into England. St. Botolf's town, Lincolnshire, is now known as Boston.

BOYD—m Scottish place-name derivation.

BRADEN—m 'Broad valley' (Old English).

BRADLEY—m 'Broad meadow' (Old English).

BRANNEN—m 'Beautiful raven' (Welsh).

BRENDA—f 'Sword' (Old Norse). Its spread attributed to Scott's use of it for a major character in *The Pirate* (1821).

BRENDAN—m 'Stinking hair' (Old Irish). Sixth-century Irish saint. Brendan Behan, twentieth-century author.

BRENT—m 'Burnt' (Old English).

BRETT—m 'Breton' (French).

BRIAN—m 'Strong' (Celtic). Derivation and meaning uncertain. Perhaps Irish in association with their national hero Brian Boru (926-1014).

BRIDGET—f 'The high one' (Celtic). Brighid was the fire goddess of the Celts. St. Brighid, Irish saint 453-523.

BRINSLEY—m Place-name derivation.

BRITANNIA—f The name of our island in ancient geography, because the Romans thought its outline looked like a woman seated on a rock. Used as a Christian name in the eighteenth century.

BRONWEN—f 'Of the white bosom' (Welsh).

BRUCE—m From the place-name Brieuse in Normandy. Robert the Bruce (1274-1329), king of Scotland.

BRUNELLA—f Diminutive form of Bruno.

BRUNO—m 'Brown' (Teutonic). There are four saints of

this name. Bruno Walter (died 1962), German-born American conductor.

BRYONY—f Flower name; climbing plant found in hedges.

BUCKLEY—m Surname derivation.

BYRNE—m 'Coat of arms' (Old English).

BYSSHE—m 'From the thicket' (Old English).

CADMUS—m 'Man from the east' (Greek).

CADWALLADER—m 'Battle-leader' (Welsh). Used in Wales from the seventh century. More common in England as a surname.

CAESAR—m 'Hairy one' (Latin). Title borne by all emperors after Julius Caesar and later as Tsar and Kaiser by Russian and German rulers. Sometimes given to boys born by Caesarean section.

CALEB—m 'Impetuous' (Hebrew). Old Testament Hebrew leader.

CALISTA—f 'Fairest' (Greek).

CALLAN—m Modern invention, after television character.

CAMERON—m 'Crooked nose' (Gaelic).

CAMILLA—f 'Attendant at a sacrifice' (Etruscan). Queen of the Volscians in Virgil's *Aeneid*. Fanny Burney's *Camilla, or a Picture of Youth* (1796) may have started its modern revival.

CANDIDA—f 'White' (Latin). Given limited popularity by Shaw's play of that name in 1898.

CARA—f 'Dear' (Italian).

CARADOC—m 'Amiable' (Welsh). Equivalent of the old British name of Caractacus, British king, son of Cymbeline who ruled at Colchester.

CAREY—m 'Dear' (Latin).

CARINA—f 'Dear' (Italian).

CARL—m An American compromise between the English Charles and the German Karl.

CARMEN—f 'Song' (Latin).

CAROL—f Short form of Caroline, spreading from the southern United States.

CAROLA—f Form of Charles. Carola Oman, historical novelist.

CAROLINE—f From Carolina, Italian feminine form of Charles which spread to Germany and was introduced to England through the popularity of George II's Queen Caroline of Brandenburg-Anspach (1727).

CAROLYN—f Form of Caroline.

CARYL—f 'The loved one' (Welsh).

CASIMIR—m 'Proclaimer of peace' (Polish). A line of Polish kings.

CASPAR—m Variant of Gaspar, one of the Three Wise Men.

CASSANDRA—f Original Greek meaning unknown. Daughter of Priam, King of Troy, in Greek legend. Cursed by Apollo that, although her prophecies would be true, no one would believe her.

CASSIDY—m 'Ingenious' (Celtic).

CATHERINE—f 'Pure' (Greek). St. Catherine, martyred in 307 by being broken on a wheel, is oddly remembered in the firework, the catherine wheel. 'No name is more universal in all countries and in all ranks partly from its own beauty of sound, partly from association . . .' C. M. Yonge.

CATHLEEN—f Irish form of Catherine.

CECIL—m 'Blind' (Latin). Originally from the great Roman family of Caecilius, but in our time from the family name of the influential Marquess of Salisbury. Cecil Rhodes (1853–1902), founder of Rhodesia.

CECILIA—f Form of Cecil. St. Cecilia, martyred about 177, is patron saint of music and poetry. William the Conqueror's daughter called thus was Abbess of Caen. Its later revival may be due to Fanny Burney's novel *Cecilia* (1782). Cecily, Cicely, Ciss and Cis are derivations and diminutives.

CEDRIC—m Apparently invented by Sir Walter Scott for one of his characters in *Ivanhoe*. He may have meant Cerdic, founder of the West Saxon kingdom. The hero of *Little Lord Fauntleroy* (1886), by Francis Hodgson Burnett.

CELESTE—f 'Heaven sent' (Latin).

CELIA—f 'Heavenly' (Latin). A modern Italian version of the Roman family name, though the English form is more likely a diminutive of Cecilia. Cousin of Rosalind in Shakespeare's *As You Like It*. Popular in poetry, e.g. Ben Jonson's 'To Celia' better known as 'Drink to me only with thine eyes . . .'

CERI—m 'Dear one' (Welsh).

CERIDWEN—f 'Fair poetry' (Welsh). Welsh goddess of poetry.

CHAD—m 'Battle' (Celtic). Normally used in conjunction with another word, e.g. Cadwallader. Perhaps popularised, particularly in USA by Walter Edmonds's circus story hero, Chad Hanna.

CHANTELLE—f (French). A modern fashion probably appealing on sound alone.

CHARIS—f 'Grace' (Greek). In Greek mythology the wife

17

of Hephaestus, personification of grace and beauty.

CHARITY—f 'Love' (Greek). Names from qualities became fashionable after the Reformation. So Faith, Hope and Charity were often used for triplets. Early contracted into Cherry, as shown by the daughter of Mr. Pecksniff in Dickens's *Martin Chuzzlewit*.

CHARLES—m 'A man' (Teutonic). Popular through the exploits of Charles the Great, otherwise Charlemagne. Ten French and fifteen Swedish rulers have borne this name. In England supporters of Charles I and Charles II gave it wide circulation. H.R.H. The Prince of Wales (Prince Charles Philip Arthur George) was born 14th November 1948.

CHARLOTTE—f Form of Charles. George III's marriage with Charlotte Sophia of Mecklenburg-Strelitz made it popular. Charlotte Bronte (1816-1855) author of *Jane Eyre*. The late Queen Salote of Tonga shows the name in its native form.

CHARLTON—m Place-name derivation. Charlton Heston, well-known film actor.

CHARMIAN—f 'A little joy' (Greek). Shakespeare chose it for a character in *Antony and Cleopatra* (1608).

CHERYL—f 'Love' (Welsh).

CHESTER—m Place-name derivation.

CHLOE—f 'Blooming' (Greek). One of the titles of Demeter, goddess of harvest. But Charlotte Mary Yonge says, 'In general, however, Chloe has been a property of pastoral poetry, and has thence descended to negroes and spaniels.'

CHLORIS—f 'Fresh as a daisy' (Greek). Goddess of flowers whom Romans called Flora.

CHRISTABEL—f 'Fair Christian' (Latin). Heroine of the old ballad of the brave knight Sir Cauline, and also of S. T. Coleridge's *Christabel* (1816). Dame Christabel Pankhurst, woman suffrage leader, daughter of Emmeline Pankhurst.

CHRISTIAN—m 'A Christian' (Latin). Though rare in English its occurrence may have been influenced by the hero of Bunyan's *Pilgrim's Progress*. Ten Danish kings were so called.

CHRISTINE, CHRISTINA—f Form of Christian. Now much more common than the male form. St. Christina, martyred 295, was a high-born Roman. Christina Rossetti (1830-94), poetess.

CHRISTMAS—m Obviously from the great Christian festival.

CHRISTOPHER—m 'Bearing Christ' (Latin). St. Christopher, an early Christian martyr, has become confused with the legendary giant who carried the infant Christ across a river, and so stands today as the patron saint of travellers. But the original meaning to early Christians was in its application to themselves—bearing Christ in their hearts. 'The sight of St. Christopher's image was thought to be a protection from sickness, earthquake, fire, or flood, for the rest of the day.'

CHRYSANDER—m 'Golden man' (Greek).

CHRYSOGON—f 'Golden girl' (Greek). Variants like Grisogon date from the earliest times.

CICELY—f Form of Cecilia.

CLARA, CLARE—f 'Bright' (Latin). In the sense of famous. St. Clare of Assissi (1199-1253) was founder of the Order of Poor Clares. Proclaimed by Pope Pius XII as patron saint of television in 1958. Actress Claire Bloom shows French form of the name.

CLARENCE—m From the dukedom of Clarence created in 1362 for Lionel, third son of Edward III, who married the heiress of Clare in Suffolk.

CLARIBEL—f 'Brightly fair' (Latin). Queen of Tunis in Shakespeare's *The Tempest*.

CLARICE—f A French version of Clare.

CLARIMOND—f 'Famous protector' (Teutonic). A further development of Clara.

CLARINDA—f Version of Clara. Popular name for a character in early drama.

CLARISSA—f Developed from the French form of Clare. *Clarissa Harlowe* by Samuel Richardson (1747) popularised the name.

CLARK—m 'Clerk' (Latin). An 'occupation' surname derivation.

CLAUD—m 'Lame' (Latin). From Claudius, name of two great Roman families.

CLAUDETTE—f French female diminutive of Claud.

CLAUDIA—f Form of Claud, common in Roman times.

CLAUDINE—f French diminutive of Claudia. Subject of a series of novels by 'Colette'.

CLEMENCE—f Form of Clement. Clemence Dane (pseudonym of Winifred Ashton) author of *Broome Stages* etc.

CLEMENT—m 'Mild' (Latin). Name of a saint, pope from 88-97, beginning a line of fourteen popes. St. Clement Danes church was built for Danish settlers in London, regarded by them as patron saint of sailors and black-smiths.

CLEMENTINE—f Form of Clement. Heroine of the song, 'O my darling Clementine'.

CLEOPATRA—f The Egyptian queen.

CLIFFORD—m Classic example of a place-name evolving as a surname and then from late Victorian times as a Christian name.

CLIFTON—m Place-name derivation.

CLINTON—m Name of at least ten places in the USA.

CLIVE—m Variation of Shropshire place-name meaning 'cliff'.

CLOTILDA—f 'Strong in battle' (Teutonic). The wife of Clovis, King of France (465-511), whom she successfully persuaded to embrace Christianity.

CLYDE—m Scottish river derivation.

CLYTIA—f 'Sunflower' (Greek).

COLETTE—f Diminutive of the French Nicole. St. Colette, died 1447, founded seventeen convents of the Coletine Poor Clares. 'Colette', pseudonym of the French novelist.

COLIN—m 'Victory of the people'. An abbreviation of Nicholas, originating in France but used in England from the thirteenth century. The Scottish Colin derives quite separately from the Gaelic for a frisky young dog.

COLLEY—m 'Black haired' (Old English).

COMFORT—f Obvious derivation.

CONAL(L)—m 'Powerful potentate' (Celtic).

CONAN—m 'High' (Celtic). One of the early bishops of London. Sir Arthur Conan Doyle (1859-1930), creator of Sherlock Holmes.

CONNOR—m 'High desire' (Irish).

CONRAD—m 'Bold friend' (Teutonic). Joseph Conrad (died 1924), Polish-born English novelist.

CONSTANCE—f 'Firm' (Latin). A saint who was daughter of Constantine the Great.

CONSTANTINE—m 'Persevering' (Latin). Constantine the Great (274-337), first Roman emperor to give official recognition to Christianity.

CORA—f 'Maiden' (Latin). Probably an American invention, appearing as the heroine of J. F. Cooper's Last of the Mohicans (1826) though Dryden uses Corah in 'Absalom and Achitophel' in 1681.

CORAL—f One of the 'precious stone' names more common in the twenties.

CORDELIA—f 'Jewel of the sea' (Celtic). Popularised by the character in Shakespeare's *King Lear*.

CORINNA, CORRINNE—f 'Maiden' (Greek). Corinna was a fifth century B.C. Greek lyric poetess whose name was used by Robert Herrick and other seventeenth-century poets. The second, French form is more popular today.

CORISANDE—f Originates in a medieval romance. Disraeli used it for a character in his *Lothair*.

CORNELIA—f Form of Cornelius. Original Cornelia of second century B.C. was a Roman matron celebrated for her accomplishments and virtues as a mother.

CORNELIUS—m 'Horned' (Latin). The great Roman family name which included Scipio. The name of the centurion converted by St. Peter.

CORNELL—m Form of Cornelius made popular by the American university.

CORRINNE—f French diminutive of Cora. See Corinna.

COSMO—m 'Order' (Greek). Cosmo de Medici (1519-1574), Grand Duke of Tuscany, one of a line of rulers of this name.

COSTIN—m Modern form of Constantine.

COURTENAY—m Place-name in the Ile de France which evolved via a surname.

CRAIG—m 'Crag' (Gaelic).

CRESSIDA—f 'Golden' (Greek). Complicated derivation from classical literature through the Troilus and Cressida legend which stretches on from Chaucer to Shakespeare.

CRISPIN—m 'With the curly hair' (Latin). Patron saint of shoemakers and one of two brothers martyred 287. His day is 25th October, the date of the battle of Agincourt.

CRYSTAL—f Developed alongside the modern gem names, but could have been influenced by the Crystal Palace put up for the 1851 Exhibition in London.

CURRAN—m 'Hero' (Celtic).

CURTIS—m From the surname. A serving man in *The Taming of the Shrew*.

CUTHBERT—m 'Shining glory' (Old English). The body of St. Cuthbert (died 687), preserved in Durham Cathedral, was reputed to have worked miracles. In First World War was used to describe those who evaded conscription.

CYNTHIA—f 'Of Mount Cynthos' (Greek). In Mrs. Gaskell's *Wives and Daughters*. Poet's name for Queen Elizabeth I.

CYPRIAN—m 'of Cyprus' (Latin). St. Cyprian, martyred at Carthage in 258.

CYRIL—m 'Lordly' (Greek). At least three saints of this name up to the ninth century, but only fashionable in Britain in the last hundred years.

CYRUS—m 'Throne' (Persian). Cyrus the Great, the founder of the Persian Empire, figures prominently in the Bible (died 529 B.C.). General Cyrus Choke was a remarkable American featured in Dickens's *Martin Chuzzlewit*.

DACRE—m Though originally inferring 'a man from Acre in Palestine' it is derived today from the great English family name.

DAFFODIL—f Modern flower name.

DAGOBERT—m 'Day-bright' (Old English).

DAISY—f Actually started life in Victorian times as a pet-name for Margaret.

DALE—m 'Valley' (Old English).

DAMARIS—f 'Calf-like' (Greek). New Testament woman converted by St. Paul.

DAMIAN, DAMON—m 'Tamer' (Greek).

DANA—f Celtic goddess of fertility.

DANIEL—m 'Whom God has judged' (Hebrew). Hero of the lions' den. Daniel Defoe (1660-1731), novelist and political journalist famous for *Robinson Crusoe*.

DAPHNE—f 'Laurel' (Greek). A nymph loved by Apollo and turned into a bush. Now used for a range of flowering shrubs.

DARBY—m 'Never envious' (Old Irish). A debased form of Diarmit which may have given rise to the 'Darby and Joan' first celebrated in verse in 1735.

DARCY—m or f Family name (D'Arcy) of one of the Conqueror's knights, remembered in the village of Tolleshunt D'Arcy, Essex.

DARLENE, DARLINE, DARALYN—f Form of Darrel.

DARREL(L), DARYL—m 'Darling' (Old English).

DAVID—m 'Beloved' (Hebrew). David who killed Goliath grew up to be second king of Israel. The patron saint of Wales (died 601).

DAWN—f Derivation obvious. A modern name from romantic writers.

DEAN—m 'Valley' (Teutonic). Surname used as forename.

DEBORAH—f 'A bee' (Hebrew). Later interpreted as 'eloquent'. A prophetess in Biblical times (Judges iv). John Milton's youngest daughter.

DECIMA—f Form of Decimus.

DECIMUS—m Tenth (Latin). Most used in Victorian families for the tenth child. Decimus Burton, nineteenth-century architect, designer of the triumphal arch at Hyde Park Corner, London.

DEIRDRE—f 'Fear' (Celtic). Much featured in Irish plays and poems.

DELANO—m 'Grove of alders' (Latin).

DELIA—f 'Of Delos' (Greek). Sometimes short for Cordelia.

DELILAH—f 'Delight' (Hebrew).

DELLA—f Diminutive of Adela or Delia.

DENISE—f Borrowed from the French as a female version of Denis.

DENNIS—m 'Of Dionysus' (Greek). The name of several saints. Can be spelt with one N.

DENZIL—m Surname converted. Denzil Holles (1599-1670), English statesman.

DEREK—m 'Ruler of the tribe' (Teutonic). Sometimes spelt Derrick. Derives from Theodoric.

DERINA—f Form of Derwin.

DERMOT—m Derives from Diarmit.

DERWIN—m 'Sincere friend' (Old English).

DESDEMONA—f 'Misery' (Greek). The heroine of Shakespeare's *Othello*.

DESIREE—f 'Desired' (French).

DESMOND—m 'South Munster' (Irish). Place-name—surname—forename evolution. Its popularity is quite unaccountable.

DIANA—f 'Goddess' (Latin). The moon goddess. Recently popular through the heroine of Scott's *Rob Roy* and Meredith's *Diana of the Crossways*. Now much more common in its French form of Diane.

DIARMIT—m 'Never envious' (Old Irish). The origin of Dermot and Darby.

DIDO—f Queen of Carthage.

DIGBY—m Place-name—surname derivation.

DILWYN—m Welsh place-name.

DILYS—f 'Genuine' (Welsh). Dilys Powell, film critic and author.

DINAH—f 'Judgement' (Hebrew). Daughter of Jacob and Leah.

DIONYSIUS—m 'Of Dionysus' (Greek). The fertility god from whom the powerful tyrant of Syracuse (died 367 B.C.) got his name. It continued into Christian times as the name of a saint and pope. Its modern form is Denis.

DIRK—m Dutch short form of Derek. Dirk Bogarde, actor.

DOLLY—f Pet name for Dorothy.

DOLORES—f 'Grief' (Spanish). Short for 'Mary of the Sorrows', i.e. the mother of Jesus.

DOMINIC—m 'Of the Lord' (Latin). Perhaps used in the sense 'of the Lord's Day', for boys born on a Sunday. Girls called Dominica. St. Dominic founded the order of preaching friars (c 1200) known as Black Friars from the colour of their habit.

DONALD—m 'Proud chief' (Celtic). Very common in Scotland where it began. Reckoned to be the name of the first Christian king of Scotland.

DORA—f Short form of Dorothy.

DORCAS—f 'Gazelle' (Greek). 'In the New Testament (Acts ix, 36) a woman who was full of good deeds, and made coats and garments for the poor; hence, a Dorcas society . . . of the women of a church who supply garments to the needy.' *(New Century Cyclopaedia of Names)*

DOREEN—f 'Gift of God' (Modern Irish). An adaptation by the Irish of Dorothy as Doirean has been re-imported to England in this form, helped, perhaps, by the popularity of Edna Lyall's novel, *Doreen* (1894).

DORIAN—m Greek place-name derivation.

DORINDA—f Eighteenth-century romantic diminutive of Dorothy, e.g. the daughter of Lady Bountiful in Farquhar's *Beaux' Stratagem*.

DORIS—f 'Sea nymph' (Greek). Noted by Dickens as a name, it then became mysteriously popular by the turn of the century.

DOROTHY, DOROTHEA—f 'Gift of God' (Greek). Often abbreviated to Dolly and further to Doll—a child's toy—because the name was so popular that 'It finally became the generic term for the wooden children that at least as late as the infancy of Elizabeth Stuart were called babies or puppets', C. M. Yonge.

DOUGAL—m 'Black stranger' (Old Irish). Character in Scott's *Rob Roy*.

DOUGLAS—m 'Dark blue' (Celtic). Originally a river name which became the title of the great Scottish family.

DRUSILLA—f Roman family name. Livia Drusilla was the second wife of Augustus and Herod named his daughter thus.

DUDLEY—m Place in Worcestershire gave the surname of the family so powerful in Tudor times, and the forename is a nineteenth-century compliment to that family.

DUFF—m 'Black hair' (Gaelic).

DULCIE—f 'Sweet' (Latin).

DUNCAN—m 'Brown warrior' (Old Irish). Two Scottish kings of the eleventh century, the first murdered by Macbeth and immortalised by Shakespeare.

DUNSTAN—m 'Of the stony hill' (Old English). St. Dunstan (924-988) became archbishop of Canterbury, patron saint of goldsmiths.

DURAND—m 'Lasting' (Latin). Occasionally shown as Durant.

DWIGHT—m Surname carried from England to America by early settlers, where it was borne by a long line of famous men and women and so, understandably, became a forename, as in Dwight D. Eisenhower, 34th President of the USA.

DYLAN—m 'Son of the wave' (Welsh). Legendary hero. Dylan Thomas (1914-1953), Welsh poet.

DYMPHNA—f 'One fit to be' (Irish).

EAMON(N)—m Irish form of Edmund.

EARL—m Example of a title taken as a forename.

EASTER—f Used to christen a child born during this festival, but in earlier days more often found because it was confused with Esther.

EBEN—m 'Stone' (Hebrew).

EBENEZER—m 'Stone of help' (Hebrew). Samuel vii. 12 tells of this stone put up by Samuel to commemorate victory over the Philistines.

EDELINA—f Diminutive of Adela.

EDEN—m or f 'Delight' (Hebrew). According to the Bible the very first place-name, and therefore a natural, though not widely used, forename.

EDGAR—m 'Royal warrior' (Old English). King of England in 959 though not crowned until 973.

EDITH—f Form of Edgar. St. Eadgyth (962-984) was the daughter of King Edgar, but in its present form it is a Victorian revival.

EDMOND, EDMUND—m 'Wealthy protector' (Teutonic). St. Edmond, King of the East Angles, martyred by the Danes in 870. Edmund the Magnificent, King of the West Saxons and Mercians, died 946.

EDNA—f 'Rejuvenation' (Hebrew). Edna Lyall, novelist writing from 1879, may have been the cause of its modern revival.

EDRIC—m 'Noble rule' (Teutonic).

EDWARD—m 'Wealthy protector' (Teutonic). Edward the Elder, son of Alfred the Great, ruled the West Saxons

901-924 and set the name of a line of kings down to Edward VIII, who abdicated in 1936.

EDWIN—m 'Gay companion' (Old English). Edwin (died 633), King of Northumbria.

EDWINA—f Modern version of Edwin. Lady Edwina Mountbatten, wife of Earl Mountbatten of Burma, died 1960.

EFFIE—f Short for Euphemia.

EGBERT—m 'Gleaming sword' (Old English). First king of England (died 839).

EGIDIA—f Derives from the Latin form of Giles.

EILEEN—f 'Light' (Greek). Development of Helen.

EINAR—m 'Warrior chief' (Old Norse).

ELAINE—f A form, in old French, of Helen popularised by Tennyson's account of Lancelot and Elaine.

ELDON—m Old English place-name derivation.

ELDRED—m Form of Aldred.

ELEANOR, ELINOR—f A form of Helen 'the bright one' (Greek). Introduced into England by Eleanor of Aquitaine, wife of Henry II, but popular through Eleanor (died 1290), queen of Edward I. Her journey to burial caused the erection of the beautiful Eleanor crosses.

ELEAZAR—m 'Helped by God' (Hebrew). The name of Aaron's eldest surviving son, and his successor as High Priest.

ELECTRA—f 'Amber' (Greek).

ELFREDA—f 'Hidden strength' (Old English). A Saxon name revived in Victorian times. Elfrida was mother of Ethelred the Unready.

ELI—m 'Of the highest' (Hebrew). The High Priest who brought up the prophet Samuel.

ELIAS—m Greek form of Elijah. The prophet Elijah is referred to in the New Testament as Elias.

ELIJAH—m 'Jehovah is God' (Hebrew). Gave rise to surname, and latterly forename, of Ellis.

ELISE—f Fashionable French form of Elizabeth.

ELISHA—m 'God's gift' (Hebrew). Prophet who succeeded Elijah.

ELIZABETH—f 'God is my all' (Hebrew). The mother of St. John the Baptist. Spelt with an 's' on the continent. Its popularity directly attributable to Queen Elizabeth I.

ELKANAH—m 'Whom God has created' (Hebrew). Father of the prophet Samuel.

ELLA—f 'Best of all' (Teutonic). Pre-Raphaelites took this medieval name and made it fashionable.

ELLARD—m 'Nobly endures' (Teutonic).

ELLEN—f Now quite independent form of Helen. Dame Ellen Terry (1848-1928), actress.

ELLERY—m 'Sweetly spoken' (Greek).

ELLIS—m Form of Elijah.

ELMA—f An American abbreviation of the Italian female form of William.

ELMER—m 'Nobly famous'. Derived from Aylmer and largely confined to the USA.

ELMO—m Corruption of Erasmus, representing, in St. Elmo's Castle, a third-century Persian saint. Also popular name of St. Peter Gonzalez (died 1246), patron saint of seamen, giving rise to the phenomenon of 'St. Elmo's fire'—an electrical discharge from the mast of a ship during a storm.

ELROY—m 'The king' (Spanish).

ELSA—f German short form of Elizabeth, now quite independent.

ELSIE, ELSPETH—f Forms of Elizabeth.

ELTON—m 'From the old settlement' (Old English).

ELVINA—f 'Wise friend' (Teutonic).

ELVIRA—f 'Wise counsel' (Teutonic). Spanish form of the ancient name from which Aubrey also developed.

ELVIS—m 'Wise one' (Teutonic).

ELWIN—m Form of Alwyn.

EMANUEL—m 'God with us' (Hebrew). The name given to Christ as deliverer of Judah—prophesied by Isaiah (vii. 14 and viii. 8).

EMERALD—f From the green precious stone, a comparatively recent innovation.

EMERY—m 'World ruler' (Teutonic).

EMILY—f 'Hard worker' (Latin). Roman family name which Chaucer used as Emelye in his 'Knight's Tale'. Emily Bronte, author of *Wuthering Heights* (1848).

EMLYN—m 'Hard worker' (Welsh). From Teutonic origin and still common in Wales. Emlyn Williams, actor and author.

EMMA—f 'Wholly true' (Teutonic). Married Ethelred the Unready in 1002. Emma Woodhouse, heroine of *Emma* by Jane Austen (1816). Emma, Lady Hamilton (1761-1815), great love of Lord Nelson.

EMMELINE—f 'Worker' (Old French). Doubtful etymology, but it is of Norman origin. Emmeline Pankhurst

(1858-1928), leader of the 'Votes for Women' movement.

EMRYS—m Welsh form of Ambrose.

ENA—f 'Little fire' (Irish). Popularised by Princess (Victoria Eugenie Julia) Ena (born 1887), who became queen of Spain. Ena Sharples, rugged character in *Coronation Street* television serial.

ENID—f 'Life' (Welsh). Used in England after Tennyson had his 'Geraint and Enid' (part of *Idylls of the King*) published in 1859. Enid Blyton (died 1968), successful children's author.

ENOCH—m 'Skilful' (Hebrew). The father of Methuselah. A book of 'Revelations' is attributed to him. 'Enoch Arden', tragic poem by Tennyson. Enoch Powell, politician.

EPHRAIM—m 'Green pastures' (Hebrew). Second son of Joseph, founded one of the twelve tribes of Israel.

ERASMUS—m 'Beloved' (Greek). Desiderius Erasmus (1465-1536), Dutch scholar of the Renaissance.

ERIC—m 'Noble ruler' (Teutonic). The meaning can only be tentative. Twenty Scandinavian kings bore this name. Eric the Red, Norse rover, founded Greenland. Revived in the nineteenth century through Dean Farrar's popular school story, *Eric; or, Little by Little* (1858).

ERICA—f Form of Eric which first occured in Edna Lyall's very popular novel *We two* (1884).

ERMINTRUDE—f 'All powerful' (Teutonic). A Victorian fashion which has died away.

ERNEST—m 'Earnestness' (Teutonic). A revival by the Victorians, perhaps through Queen Victoria's uncle, Ernest I of Saxe-Coburg-Gotha.

ERNESTINE—f Form of Ernest.

ERROL—m 'Wanderer' (Latin). Based today on popularity of screen hero Errol Flynn.

ESAU—m 'Blind' (Hebrew). The elder son of Isaac, twin brother of Jacob, to whom he sold his birthright 'for a mess of pottage'.

ESDRAS—m 'Help' (Hebrew).

ESME—m or f 'Beloved' (French). Came to England from France via Scotland.

ESMERALDA—f Spanish form of Emerald. Character in Hugo's *Hunchback of Notre Dame*.

ESMOND—m 'Gracious protection' (Old English). Thackeray's *The History of Henry Esmond* (1852) could account for its modern revival.

ESPERANCE—f 'Hope' (French).

ESTELLE—f 'Star' (French). The heroine of Dickens's *Great Expectations*.

ESTHER—f 'Myrtle' (Persian). One of the books of the Old Testament. Oratorio by Handel based on Racine's play *Esther*.

ESWEN—f 'Strength' (Welsh).

ETHAN—m 'Never failing stream' (Hebrew). The title of Psalm 89. Ethan Allen, American revolutionary figure, made it popular in the USA.

ETHEL—f 'Noble' (Old English). A component of Saxon names which finally became used separately.

ETHELDRED(A)—f 'Noble maiden' (Old English). St. Etheldreda (died 769) was queen of Northumbria, founder of a convent at Ely where the cathedral was built over her remains. This name connects with Audrey.

ETHELINDA—f 'Noble serpent' (Teutonic).

ETHELRED—m 'Noble counsel' (Old English). King of Wessex (866-871) and brother of Alfred. Ethelred, son of Edgar, was king of England 978-1016, and called the Unready—a pun on his name meaning 'un-counselled'.

EUDO—m 'Child' (Old Norse). Introduced by the Normans.

EUGENE—m 'Well-born' (Greek). A line of popes from the seventh century. Made popular by the exploits of Prince Eugen of Savoy (1663-1736), the military strategician. *Eugene Onegin*—opera by Tchaikovsky.

EUGENIE, EUGENIA—f Form of Eugene. Empress Eugenie (1826-1920) of France, wife of Napoleon III.

EULALIA—f 'Sweetly-speaking' (Greek). Largely confined to the south-west of England.

EUNICE—f 'Auspicious victory' (Greek). The mother of Timothy (2 Tim. i. 5).

EUPHEMIA—f 'Fair speech' (Greek). A virgin-martyr of Bithynia.

EURWYN—m 'Golden' (Welsh).

EUSTACE—m 'Fruitful' (Greek). Patron saint of huntsmen.

EUSTACIA—f Form of Eustace.

EVADNE—f 'Fortunate' (Greek).

EVAN—m Welsh form of John.

EVANDER—m 'Well-doer' (Greek).

EVANGELINE—f Invention attributed to Henry Longfellow for the heroine of his poem 'Evangeline' (1847).

EVE, EVA—f 'Lively' (Hebrew). In the Bible, the first woman, the mother of the human race. Little Eva in *Uncle*

Tom's Cabin (1852) had considerable influence on its use.

EVELINA—f 'Pleasant' (Teutonic). Revived by Fanny Burney for her novel of that name in 1778.

EVELYN—m or f 'Hazel' (Latin). Said to be connected with the French for hazel-nut, which was the Celtic symbol of wisdom. This gave rise to the surname, as in John Evelyn, seventeenth-century diarist, from which the forename developed.

EVERARD—m 'Tough as a bear' (Teutonic). Everard Webley, character in Huxley's *Point Counter Point* (1928).

EVERIL—f Form of Averil.

EWEN, EWAN—m 'Well-born' (Celtic). Though more in favour in Scotland it was once common in England too.

EZEKIEL—m 'May God strengthen' (Hebrew). Hebrew prophet.

EZRA—m 'Help' (Hebrew). Hebrew scribe and priest, author of one of the books of the Old Testament.

FABIAN—m Roman family name of which the original meaning is obscure. Third century pope and martyr.

FABIOLA—f Diminutive form of Fabian.

FAITH—f Not used until after the Reformation, but now considered old-fashioned.

FARLEY—m 'Further meadow' (Old English). Place name derivation as in Farley Mount.

FAY—f 'Fairy'. May have started out as a pet-name for Faith.

FELICITY—f 'Happiness' (Latin). One of the many abstract names which became popular from the seventeenth century.

FELIX—m 'Happy' (Latin). St. Felix, East Anglian apostle, gave Felixstowe, Suffolk, its name. There are over fifty saints who bear this name.

FENELLA—f 'She of the white shoulder' (Gaelic). Character in Scott's *Peveril of the Peak*. Fenella Fielding, actress.

FERDINAND—m 'Venturesome' (Teutonic). Borne by many kings of Castile. Ferdinand de Lesseps (1805-1894), architect of the Suez Canal.

FERGUS—m 'The chosen man' (Old Irish). Fergus I was in legend the first Irish king of Scotland sometime in the sixth century.

FERN—f Plant name.

FIDEL—m 'Faithful' (Latin). Fidel Castro of Cuba.

FIONA—f 'Fair' (Gaelic). Tentative derivation of name

probably invented by William Sharp (1855-1905) for his character 'Fiona Macleod'.

FLETCHER—m 'Arrow-maker' (French). A modern derivation from the surname.

FLEUR—f 'Flower' (French). Recent revival through television production of Galsworthy's *The Forsyte Saga*.

FLORA—f 'Goddess of flowers' (Latin). St. Flora was martyred in Spain in 850. Flora Macdonald (1722-1790), Scottish Jacobite heroine, made it popular in that country.

FLORENCE—m or f 'Blooming' (Latin). More common today as a girl's name. Florence Nightingale (1820-1912) gave this name its greatest boost.

FLORETTA—f 'Little flower' (Latin).

FLOYD—m English adaptation of the Welsh Lloyd.

FORD—m River and place-name derivation influenced by Henry Ford, the famous car-maker.

FRANCES, FRANCESCA—f 'A Frenchwoman' (Italian). Form of Francis. Madame D'Arblay (1752-1840) is better known as Frances (Fanny) Burney—author of several famous novels.

FRANCIS—m 'Frenchman' (Latin). Further derived from the fact that even under the Romans there were men who considered themselves 'franks' or free men. Rulers of France, Austria and Sicily have been thus named. Francis of Assissi (1182-1226), Italian monk and preacher, was founder of the order of Franciscans.

FRANCOISE—f French form of Frances.

FRANK—m Short form of Francis but now sometimes used in its own right.

FREDA—f Form of Winifred.

FREDERIC(K)—m 'Peaceful ruler' (Teutonic). Frederick the Great (1712-1786), created the state of Prussia.

FREDERICA—f Victorian female form of Frederic.

FREYA—f 'Lady' (Norse).

FRUSANNAH—f Artificial combination of Frances and Susannah; pet form is Frusie.

FULBERT—m 'Very bright' (Teutonic).

FULK—m 'People's warrior' (Teutonic). Sir Fulke Greville (1554-1628), English poet and statesman.

FULVIA—f 'Tawny-coloured' [hair] (Latin).

GABRIEL—m 'Strong man of God' (Hebrew). The archangel who announced to Zachariah the birth of his son John the Baptist, and to the Virgin Mary the birth of Jesus Christ. Gabriel Fahrenheit, who introduced the mercury thermometer, was born 1686.

GABRIELLE—f Form of Gabriel from France.

GAIL—f Short form of Abigail.

GALFRIDA—f Form of Geoffrey in its original Latin.

GAMALIEL—m 'God's reward' (Hebrew). Underlining the value of a male child in early communities.

GARDENIA—f Flower name of recent introduction.

GARETH—m Arose from a mistake by Malory in his writing of a Welsh name for a character in his *Morte d'Arthur* and repeated by Tennyson in his *Gareth and Lynnet* which made it popular.

GARNET—m or f From the precious stone. First Viscount, Garnet Joseph Wolseley, British general up to 1900, gave rise to the saying 'All Sir Garnet . . .'

GARY—m Possibly from Gerard. Gary Cooper, film actor.

GASTON—m 'Man of Gascony' (French). Fairly common French name which has some currency in Britain.

GAVIN—m 'Battle hawk' (Welsh). Originally from Gawain, but now more common in Scotland in this form.

GAY—f Modern 'abstract virtue' name.

GAYLORD—m 'Jolly' (French).

GEMMA—f 'Precious stone' (Italian).

GENE—m Short-form of Eugene.

GENEVIEVE—f 'White wave' (Celtic). Heroine of Coleridge's poem, 'Love'. Title of a film about a veteran car which, strangely enough, may account for a modest revival. Saint Geneviève of Brabant was eighth-century heroine of later legends.

GEOFFREY—m 'Pledge of peace' (Teutonic). Geoffrey Chaucer (died 1400) achieved immortality with his *Canterbury Tales*.

GEORGE—m 'Tiller of the soil' (Greek). St. George, patron saint of England, was a Roman military tribune martyred in 303. His dragon-killing was legendary. The House of Hanover gave Britain royal Georges for 116 years and brought the name thoroughly into favour.

GEORGIANA, GEORGINA—f Form of George. Lady Georgiana Spencer (born 1757) was a beauty painted by both Reynolds and Gainsborough.

GERAINT—m 'Old' (Welsh). Originally Latin.

GERALD—m 'Straight as a spear' (Teutonic).

GERALDINE—f Form of Gerald said to have been invented by Henry Howard, Earl of Surrey, about 1540 in his poems concerning Lady Elizabeth Fitzgerald.

GERARD—m 'Spear sharp' (Teutonic). Gerard the Blessed

founded the Order of Hospitallers of Saint John of Jerusalem in 1080.

GERBOLD—m 'Bold spear' (Teutonic).

GERDA—f 'Emblem of peace and blessing' (Old Norse). Wife of the Norse god Freyr. Popularised in this century by Hans Christian Andersen's use of it in *The Snow Queen.*

GERMAINE—f 'Of Germany' (Latin).

GERTRUDE—f 'Spear-strong' (Teutonic). Seventh-century St. Gertrude of Nivelles became patron saint of travellers. Gertrude, Queen of Denmark and mother of Hamlet in Shakespeare's play.

GERVAIS, GERVASE—m 'Henchman' (Teutonic). Gervase of Canterbury and Gervase of Tilbury were medieval English chroniclers.

GERWYN—m 'Fair love' (Welsh).

GETHIN—m 'Dark-skinned' (Welsh).

GIDEON—m 'Having only a stump for a hand' (Hebrew). Hebrew religious reformer.

GILBERT—m 'Honour bright' (Teutonic). St. Gilbert (thirteenth century) was last Scotsman to be canonised.

GILDA—f 'Golden' (Teutonic).

GILES—m 'Kid' (Greek). Possibly meant, in extension, 'wearer of a goat-skin'.

GILLIAN—f Popular English form of Julian, was once used to describe a flirt and so 'to jilt'.

GILMOUR—m 'Servant of Mary' (mother of Jesus) (Gaelic). Developed from the surname.

GINA—f Short form of Georgina.

GINETTE—f French origin, meaning unknown, appearing in birth announcements in recent years.

GISELA—f 'Honourable' (Teutonic).

GLADYS—f (Welsh) Appears from time immemorial as the Welsh (Gwladys) version of the Latin Claudia. Its revival in England is only from the last century.

GLEN—m 'From the valley' (Celtic).

GLENDA—f 'Good' (Welsh).

GLORIA—f 'Glory' (Latin). Of late Victorian origin.

GLYNIS—f 'Little valley' (Welsh).

GODDARD—m 'Strong through God' (Teutonic).

GODFREY—m 'Peace of God' (Teutonic).

GODIVA—f 'God's gift' (Old English). Heroine of the Coventry ride, who lived in the eleventh century.

GODRIC—m 'Ruling through God' (Old English).

GODWIN—m 'God's champion' (Old English). Godwin(e),

Earl of the West Saxons, who died in 1053, was father of King Harold.

GOLDWIN—m 'Valued friend' (Old English).

GORDON—m Originally from the Scottish family name, but its use as a forename received impetus from the career of General Gordon (1833-85).

GORONWY—m 'Hero' (Welsh).

GRACE—f 'Grace' (Latin).

GRACILIA—f 'Slender' (Latin).

GRAHAM—m Very popular recent adoption of an old Scottish family name.

GRANT—m 'Great' (Old French).

GREGORY—m 'The watchful one' (Greek). Two early fathers of the Eastern church and a line of sixteen popes from St. Gregory the Great.

GRENVILLE—m French family name from which came the great English family of statesmen.

GRETA—f A Swedish version of a pet form of Margaret. Greta Garbo, actress.

GRIFFIN, GRIFFITH—m 'Old warrior' (Welsh).

GRIMBALD—m 'Fierce and bold' (Old English). A monk of St. Omer, established in Oxford by King Alfred to promote learning there, became a Saxon saint.

GRISELDA—f 'I fight for Christ' (Teutonic). Interpretation of original meaning is tentative. Chaucer told Griselda's story in his 'Clerk's Tale'.

GRISWOLD—m 'Christ's power' (Teutonic).

GUNTER—m 'Bold in battle' (Teutonic). Gunter Grass, modern German author.

GUSTAV(US)—m 'Scholar's staff' (Teutonic). Made popular through line of Swedish kings of this name from 1523 down to recent times. Gustav Holst (1874-1934), English musician.

GUY—m 'Broad' (Teutonic). Latinised as Guido. The notorious Guy Fawkes caused a hiatus in its use until modern times when it became a favourite in magazine stories. Thomas Guy, bookseller, founded Guy's Hospital in 1722.

GWENDA—f Pet-name for Gwendolen.

GWENDOLEN, GWENDOLINE—f 'White-browed' (Welsh). Appears in Arthurian legend.

GWYN(N)ETH—f 'Bliss' (Welsh).

GWYNFOR—m 'Fair place' (Welsh).

HACON—m 'Right-hand man' (Old Norse). As Haakon, represents a line of kings of Norway stretching back to 934.

HADWIN—m 'Family friend' (Teutonic).

HAL—m Form of Henry.

HAM—m 'From the hot lands' (Hebrew). Originated from the progenitor of the Hamites who lived in the south. Ham was the son of Noah.

HAMILTON—m Scottish place-name.

HAMISH—m Gaelic form of James, said to have been popularised by William Black (1841-98), who often used the name for characters in his novels.

HAMON—m 'Home-lover' (Teutonic). Gave rise to Hamlet, Hamblin and other surnames. Shakespeare's *Hamlet* is, however, from the Icelandic.

HANNAH—f 'Favoured by God' (Hebrew). The mother of the prophet Samuel.

HANNIBAL—m 'The grace of Baal' (Phoenician). Hannibal (died c 183 B.C.), the great Carthaginian general. His name was a favourite in Cornwall in earlier times, which may have been due to the trade in tin with the Phoenicians.

HARCOURT—m French place-name.

HARMONIA—f 'Unifying' (Greek).

HAROLD—m 'Leader of men' (Old English). Harold Godwinson lost the throne of England to William the Conqueror.

HARRIET—f Form of Harry and so deriving from Henry. Often abbreviated to Hatty. Harriet Beecher-Stowe wrote *Uncle Tom's Cabin* (1851).

HARTLEY—m Place-name—surname derivation.

HARVEY—m 'Battleworthy' (Old Breton).

HAWIS—f 'Worth fighting for' (Teutonic). Common enough in the twelfth century to give rise to the surname Hawes.

HAYDN, HAYDEN—m 'Fire' (Celtic).

HAYLEY—f Surname origin. Hayley Mills, actress.

HAZEL—m or f One of the Victorian plant and flower names which had such meteoric rise to popularity.

HEATHER—f Plant name of Victorian vintage.

HEBE—f 'Youth' (Greek). Greek goddess of youth and cup-bearer to the gods.

HECTOR—m 'Standfast' (Greek). Son of Priam, defender of Troy, killed by Achilles.

HEDDA—f 'Strife battle' (Teutonic).

HEIDI—f Title of the world-famous children's book by Johanna Spyri (1881) which gave currency to the name.

HELEN(A)—f 'The bright one' (Greek). Helen of Troy,

wife of Menelaus, King of Sparta. St. Helena (died 338) was reputed daughter of Cunobelin (Old King Cole) and mother of the Emperor Constantine.

HELGA—f 'Holy' (Norse).

HELIANTHE—f 'Sunflower' (Greek).

HENGIST—m 'Like a stallion' (Teutonic).

HENRIETTA—f Form of Henry brought to England by Henriette Marie, wife of Charles I.

HENRY—m 'Head of the house' (Teutonic). William the Conqueror's youngest son, and a long line of English kings down to Henry VIII.

HEPHZIBAH—f 'My delight is in her' (Hebrew). The wife of Hezekiah, King of Judah about 700 B.C. Hephzibah Menuhin, pianist and sister of violinist Yehudi.

HERA—f 'Lady' (Greek).

HERBERT—m 'Outstanding' (Teutonic). Early name which fell into neglect until the turn of the century, when its revival may have been a compliment to the noble family of that name.

HERCULES—m 'Noble fame' (Greek). Original meaning is tentative. Name of the son of Zeus, and of a constellation.

HEREWARD—m 'Protector' (Old English). Hereward the Wake, Saxon guerrilla leader against William the Conqueror. Subject of the novel of that name by Charles Kingsley (1866).

HERMAN—m 'One of the gang' (Teutonic). Not so popular since the Second World War when it was associated with Hermann Goering.

HERMIA—f Derived from Hermes, messenger to the Greek gods, but today's source of inspiration is the character in Shakespeare's *A Midsummer Night's Dream*.

HERMIONE—f Form of Hermes used by Shakespeare for his queen in *A Winter's Tale*. In ancient legend, wife of Cadmus, founder of Thebes.

HERO—f 'Heavenly' (Greek). From the goddess Hera. The great love of Leander in the classical legend. English use may well date from its appearance in Shakespeare's *Much Ado About Nothing*.

HESTER—f Latin version of Esther.

HEZEKIAH—m 'God is my strength' (Hebrew). King of Judah, c 700 B.C.

HIBERNIA—f 'Ireland' (Latin).

HILARY—m or f 'Cheerful' (Latin). St. Hilarius of Poitiers died 368. Hilaire Belloc (1870-1953), author, shows French form.

HILDA—f 'Battle-maiden' (Old English). St. Hilda (614-80) founded Whitby Abbey in 657. Revived in the nineteenth century.

HILDEBRAND—m 'A sword in the strife' (Teutonic). St. Hildebrand (1000-1085) was Pope Gregory VII.

HILDEGARDE—f 'Tried in battle' (Teutonic). St. Hildegard, abbess and founder of the convent of Rupertsberg in 1148.

HIPPOLYTA—f Form of Hippolytus. Name of the queen of the Amazons, as shown in *A Midsummer Night's Dream*

HIPPOLYTUS—m 'Letting horses loose' (Greek). Son of Theseus and Hippolyta, queen of the Amazons. Ippollitts in Hertfordshire is called thus after the dedication of its church to St. Hippolytus, a Roman martyred in 252.

HIRAM—m 'God is my brother' (Hebrew). Short for Ahiram, name of a king of Tyre in Old Testament times.

HOLDEN—m 'Gracious' (Teutonic).

HOLLY—f Plant name, especially for Christmas children.

HOMER—m Poet (before 700 B.C.) who wrote the *Iliad* and the *Odyssey*. It has limited use in the USA.

HONOR, HONORIA—f 'Of good repute' (Latin). This is the origin of the more common Nora.

HONOUR—f One of the abstract quality names popular after the Reformation.

HOPE—f Abstract quality name, of obvious derivation.

HORACE, HORATIO—m Roman family name. Horatius Cocles was the Roman who defended the bridge over the Tiber against the invading Etruscans. Quintus Horatius Flaccus—'Horace'—son of a freed Roman slave, became one of the great Latin poets. Horatio, 1st Viscount Nelson (1758-1805), beat the French at Trafalgar.

HORTENSIA—f Form of Hortensius.

HORTENSIUS—m 'Gardener' (Latin). A Roman family name.

HOSANNA—m or f 'Save now' (Hebrew). The crowd's cry to Jesus on his last entry into Jerusalem.

HOWARD—m 'Guardian of my heart' (Teutonic). English use derived much later from the great family surname.

HOWELL—m 'Eminent' (Welsh).

HUBERT—m 'Joyous spirit' (Teutonic). St. Hubert, Bishop of Liége in 708, is patron saint of huntsmen.

HUGH—m 'Great-hearted' (Teutonic). Latinised as Hugo. St. Hugh of Lincoln lived in the twelfth century.

HUGO—m Latinised form of Hugh.

HUMBERT—m 'Amiable giant' (Teutonic).

HUMPHREY—m 'Peaceful giant' (Teutonic). 'From being a noble and knightly name, Humphrey, as we barbarously spell it, came to be a peasant's appellation, and now is almost disused.' C. M. Yonge, 1884.

HYACINTH—m or f 'Purple' (Greek). Flower name now most commonly female.

HYWEL—m 'Eminent' (Welsh).

IAN—m Scottish form of John.

IANTHE—f 'The violet flower' (Greek). Pronounced like 'dainty'. Ianthe Eliza was the daughter of Shelley and Harriet Westbrook.

IDA—f 'Worker' (Teutonic). Its revival has been attributed to its use by Tennyson for *The Princess* (1847), which was used as the basis for Gilbert and Sullivan's *Princess Ida* (1884).

IDRIS—m 'Fiery lord' (Welsh). Cader Idris, the mountain, was so named as the legendary home of Idris the Giant, a mythical magician in Celtic lore. Idris I, first king (from 1951) of the united kingdom of Libya.

IGNATIA—f 'Fiery one' (Latin).

IGOR—m 'Husbandman' (Russian). Originally from the Norse. Prince Igor (1150-1202), great Russian hero.

IMOGEN—f Heroine of Shakespeare's *Cymbeline*. He probably intended to write Innogen as in Holinshed's *Chronicles*—the source of his inspiration. Walter de la Mare wrote the poem, 'To Imogen'.

INEZ—f Spanish form of Agnes.

INGRAM—m 'Bold as the raven' (Teutonic). Derivation from the surname.

INGRID—f 'Brought by the angels' (Old Norse). Most influenced by Ingrid Bergman, Swedish-born actress.

INIGO—m Its original Greek meaning now unknown. Inigo Jones (1573-1652), English architect.

IRA—m 'The stallion' (Aramaic). One of the priests of King David of Israel.

IRENE—f 'Peace' (Greek). Eighth-century Byzantine empress. Late use in England although it was the name of four early saints.

IRIS—f 'The rainbow' (Greek). Another example of the flower names which were so popular by the end of the last century.

IRVING—m Form of Irwin.

IRWIN—m 'Respected friend' (Old English).

ISAAC—m 'Laugh with me' (Hebrew). Literally translated 'God may laugh', because Sarah laughed when told that she would bear Isaac. Sir Isaac Newton (1642-1727) first propounder of the principle of gravity. Izaak Walton (1593-1683); the 'father of angling', and author of *The Compleat Angler*.

ISABEL(LA)—f Interchangeable with Elizabeth of which it is a French variant. Isabella Beaton wrote the famous cookery book.

ISADORA—f Form of Isidore. Isadora Duncan (1878-1927), 'American esthetic dancer', was an eccentric of her time.

ISAIAH—m 'God is generous' (Hebrew). Hebrew prophet.

ISIDORE—m 'God's gift' (Greek). St. Isidore of Seville (died 636), Spanish encyclopaedist and bishop.

ISRAEL—m 'May God prevail' (Hebrew). The name given to Jacob after he overcame the angel (Genesis xxxii, 28): thus the twelve tribes of Israel were named after his sons.

IVAN—m Scottish form of Ivo. The name of a line of dukes of Moscow, later tsars of Russia, including Ivan the Terrible (1530-1584).

IVO—m 'Archer' (Teutonic). A name which came over with the Conqueror as the French Yves, already common in heroic literature.

IVOR—m 'Bow bearer' (Teutonic). From the Old Norse name of tenth-century Danish kings of Dublin.

IVY—f Recent flower name.

JABEZ—m 'Sorrow' (Hebrew). Indicating that the child was born during some period of distress for family or tribe.

JACINTH—f 'Purple' (Greek). Name of a precious stone from the Greek for hyacinth.

JACK—m Short for John. Used independently even from medieval times.

JACOB—m 'Taking by the heel' (Hebrew). Referring originally to the manner of birth of one of the twin sons of Isaac and Rebecca, and who ousted his brother Esau.

JACQUELINE—f Feminine and diminutive form of the French Jacques, English James.

JACQUETTA—f Feminine diminutive of Jacques (James). Jacquetta Hawkes, archaeologist.

JAMES—m Actually derives from Jacob, splitting from it as a completely separate name so early that the reason is unknown. Jacob was retained as the name of the Old Testament tribal leader and James was used for the two apostles of the New Testament. Borne by five kings of Scotland and two of both England and Scotland.

JAN—m Form of John when spoken in dialect, particularly West Country. Jan Ridd was the hero of Blackmore's *Lorna Doone*.

JANE—f A rendering of Joan very common in the eighteenth and nineteenth centuries.

JANET—f Diminutive of Jane.

JAPHET—m 'May his tribe increase' (Hebrew). Third son of Noah, reputed ancestor of the Indo-European race.

JARVIS—m Form of Gervais.

JASON—m Meaning unknown. In Greek legend, leader of the Argonauts in their quest for the Golden Fleece.

JASPER—m 'Keeper of the treasure' (Persian). An alternative form of Gaspar, one of the Three Wise Men who went to Bethlehem to pay homage to the infant Jesus.

JAY—m Modern derivation from the bird or from the phonetic spelling of the letter J.

JEAN—f A modern Scottish form through Jane, of Joan. Jean Armour married Robert Burns in 1788.

JED—m Short form of Jedidiah, 'Friend of God' (Hebrew). One of the names applied to Solomon.

JEFFERY, JEFFREY—m Form of Geoffrey.

JEMIMA—f 'Dove' (Hebrew). One of the three daughters of Job.

JENNA—f Diminutive form of Jane now gaining popularity.

JENNIFER—f Cornish form of Guinevere, wife of King Arthur.

JENNY—f Pet-name for Jane or short form of Jennifer which has been used in its own right, e.g. Jenny Lind (1820-1887) 'The Swedish Nightingale'.

JEREMIAH—m 'May God exalt' (Hebrew). Second of the greater prophets of Israel.

JEREMY—m Form of Jeremiah. Jeremy Bentham (1748-1832), political philosopher.

JERMYN—m 'German' (Latin).

JEROME—m 'Holy name' (Greek). St. Jerome (340-420) translated the Bible into the vulgar language (Latin) of the time, and it is still called the Vulgate Bible. Jerome K. Jerome (died 1927), author of *Three Men in a Boat*, etc.

JESSE—m 'God exists' (Hebrew). Father of David, King of Israel.

JESSICA—f 'He beholds' (Hebrew). Of ancient lineage, but its modern use is traced to Shakespeare's *Merchant of Venice*.

JESSIE—f Though obviously a short form of Jessica its true origin is as a pet-name for Janet.

JETHRO—m 'Abundant virtues' (Hebrew). Jethro Tull (1674-1741), farmer and writer on agriculture.

JEWEL—f A 'precious stone' name.

JILL—f Form of Gillian now quite independent.

JOACHIM—m 'May God exalt' (Hebrew). Reputed father of the Virgin Mary.

JOAN—f Form of John. 'By the sixteenth century it was the third commonest English female name.'

JOANNA, JOHANNA—f A medieval rendering into Latin of Joan, re-introduced in the eighteenth century.

JOB—m 'Persecuted' (Hebrew). Not in common use. Hero of the Old Testament.

JOCASTA—f 'Moonbright' (Greek).

JOCELYN, JOSCELIN—m or f 'One of the Gothic clan' (Teutonic). Its use as a girl's name is very modern.

JOEL—m 'Jehova is God' (Hebrew). Introduced into England by the Normans.

JOHN—m 'Whom God favours' (Hebrew). John the Baptist was cousin and forerunner of Jesus. St. John, author of the fourth Gospel. There have been at least 23 popes of this name and an infinite number of rulers of countries all round the world. 'John Bull' represents the typical Englishman.

JOLYON—m A form of Julian. A character in Galsworthy's *Forsyte Saga*.

JONAH, JONAS—m 'Dove' (Hebrew). Hebrew prophet featuring in the story of the whale.

JONATHAN—m 'God's gift' (Hebrew). Son of King Saul. His particular friendship with David gave the phrase 'a David and Jonathan' to describe close companions.

JONQUIL—f Flower name of modern use.

JORAM—m 'The Lord is exulted' (Hebrew).

JORDAN—m From the holy river, probably because the child was baptised in water brought especially from that river.

JOSEPH—m 'God granted' (Hebrew). Husband of the Virgin Mary.

JOSEPHINE—f Form of Joseph. Napoleon's Empress

Josephine started the modern interest. It is the origin of Fifi.

JOSHUA—m 'God is my strength' (Hebrew). Jesus is a form of this name. Joshua succeeded Moses and led the Israelites to the Promised Land. Sir Joshua Reynolds was first president of the Royal Academy (1768).

JOSIAH—m 'Bring healing' (Hebrew). King of Judah about 600 B.C. Josiah Wedgwood (1730-1795) was the famous potter.

JOY—f Originally denoting the emotion felt by a mother on the birth of her baby.

JOYCE—m or f First appears in Celtic as Jodoc—a seventh century Breton saint. Used for men at first but now largely a feminine preserve, perhaps through the heroine of Edna Lyall's very popular *In the Golden Days* (1885).

JUDE—m 'Guided by God' (Hebrew). Judah, leader of the tribe which later formed the kingdom, is the origin of the word Jew. As Judas its connection with Iscariot made it most unpopular. Today's revival of interest may be based on the film and television production of Thomas Hardy's *Jude the Obscure*.

JUDITH—f 'A Jewess' (Hebrew). The wife of Esau. King Aethelwulf (died 878) married Judith, daughter of Charles the Bald. Short form Judy.

JULIA—f Form of Julius. Daughter of Julius Caesar. Appears in Shakespeare's *Two Gentlemen of Verona*. Robert Herrick addressed many of his poems to 'Julia'.

JULIAN—m Form of Julius. St. Julian the Hospitaller is one of the patron saints of travellers.

JULIANA—f Form of Julian. Juliana Berners—fifteenth century prioress said to have written the *Boke of St. Albans*, one of the earliest books on hunting and fishing.

JULIE—f Diminutive of Julia.

JULIET—f Remote form of Julius. Its popularity entirely due to Shakespeare's *Romeo and Juliet*.

JULIETTE—f French form of Juliet.

JULIUS—m 'Fluffy-haired' (Greek). Great Roman family name, e.g. Caius Julius Caesar. Sir Julius Caesar was the adopted name of an Italian physician to Queen Elizabeth I.

JUNE—f Name of the month. A recent innovation.

JUSTIN—m 'Just' (Latin). Name of two Byzantine emperors. St. Justin, philosopher of second century.

42

JUSTINA—f Form of Justin. A fourth-century saint.

JUSTINIAN—m Derives from Justin. Sixth and seventh century Byzantine emperors.

KAREN—f Form of Catherine, from Denmark and now surprisingly popular.

KATHERINE—f Variant of Catherine.

KATHLEEN—f Irish form of Catherine.

KATRINA—f A form of Catherine.

KAY—f Pet-name for Catherine now used independently.

KEAN—m 'Warrior' (Manx).

KEITH—m 'Of the wood' (Gaelic). Originally a place-name.

KENELM—m 'Warrior brave' (Old English). King of Mercia murdered in 819 and canonised.

KENNETH—m 'Comely' (Gaelic). First king of Scotland (died 860).

KENRICK—m 'Royal ruler' (Old English). Second king of Wessex.

KERENHAPPUCH—f 'Horn of stibium' (Hebrew). Modern meaning is 'pot of eye-makeup'! Often shortened to Keren. Refers to predilection of one of the daughters of Job who was given this name.

KERRY—m 'Dark' (Celtic).

KETURAH—f 'Fragrance' (Hebrew).

KEVIN—m 'Beautiful birth' (Old Irish). An Irish saint, sixth-century abbot of Glendalough.

KEZIAH—f 'Cinnamon' (Hebrew). One of the daughters of Job. ·

KIM—m or f Short form of Kimball, 'war-chief' (Celtic), which is now used independently.

KIRSTY—f Short form of Christian or Christiana.

KITTY—f Form of Catherine, but as Kit could be of Christopher.

LACHLAN—m 'Warlike' (Gaelic).

LAETITIA—f Form of Lettice. Name of asteroid no. 39.

LALAGE—f 'Merry talk' (Greek).

LAMBERT—m 'Of the bright land' (Teutonic). Lambert Simnel (1475-1537) was pretender to the throne of England.

LANCE—m Short form of Lancelot.

LANCELOT—m 'Of the home land' (Teutonic). One of the most famous legendary Knights of the Round Table. Lancelot ('Capability') Brown, famous landscape gardener in the eighteenth century.

LANGLEY—m 'Long meadow' (Old English). Developed from the common place-name.

LAURA—f Probably derives from Lawrence. The subject

of Petrarch's sonnets of the fourteenth century. Dame Laura Knight, contemporary painter and etcher.

LAUREN—f Variant of Laura.

LAURENCE, LAWRENCE—m 'Of the city of Laurentum' (Latin). But could be from the laurel—symbol of the conquering hero. St. Laurence, Christian martyr in 258.

LAVINIA—f 'Of Lavinium' (Latin). A town near Rome. Lavinia was the second wife of Aeneas. Thomson's translation of the book of Ruth quoted her as 'the lovely young Lavinia' and brought it into favour.

LEAH—f 'Cow' (Hebrew). First wife of Jacob.

LEE—m Short form of Leo or from the surname.

LEIGH—m 'Meadow' (Teutonic). Leigh Hunt (1784-1859), essayist and poet.

LEILA—f From the name of the heroine of the popular Persian tale 'Leila and Majnun'.

LEMUEL—m 'A man for God' (Hebrew). A king mentioned in Proverbs. The hero (Lemuel Gulliver) of Swift's *Gulliver's Travels*.

LENA—f Short form of Helen.

LENNOX—m Chieftain (Celtic).

LEO—m 'Lion' (Latin). The name of six emperors of Constantinople and thirteen popes.

LEONARD—m 'Bold as a lion' (Teutonic). The patron saint of prisoners. Leonardo da Vinci, great Italian painter and inventor.

LEONIE—f French form of Leo.

LEONORA—f Form of Eleanor introduced from the continent after the popularity of Beethoven's opera *Fidelio* which was first called Leonora after its heroine.

LEOPOLD—m 'One of the bold' (Teutonic). Victorian use through the queen's uncle Leopold, King of the Belgians, after whom she named her third son.

LEROY—m 'The king' (French).

LESLEY—f Form of Leslie. Burns wrote the poem 'Bonnie Lesley' to Miss Lesley Baillie.

LESLIE—m or f Deriving through a surname from a place-name.

LESTER—m Originally a place-name.

LETTICE—f 'Gladness' (Latin). A form of the original Latin Laetitia. Lettice Knollys was wife of the Earl of Essex in Elizabeth I's reign.

LETTY—f Diminutive of Alethia or Lettice.

LEVI—m 'Promised' (Hebrew). Third son of Jacob and Leah.

LEWIS, LOUIS—m 'Far-famed warrior' (Teutonic). As Louis,

French kings from Louis the Pious, born 778 to Louis-Phillippe, died in exile in 1850. Lewis Carroll, author of *Alice's Adventures in Wonderland* (1865).

LIAM—m Irish form of William.

LILAC—f Modern use of old plant-name.

LILIAN, LILLY, LILLAH—f Forms of Elizabeth, though found separate from an early date; modern parents may have the lily in mind.

LILIAS—f Form of Lilian. Daughter of Rider Haggard, authoress in her own right.

LILITH—f 'Goddess of storms' (Assyro-Babylonian).

LINCOLN—m English place-name—surname derivation.

LINDA—f 'Lithe as a serpent' (Teutonic).

LINDO—m 'The gentle man' (Teutonic).

LINDSAY—m or f Place-name origin, but re-imported as a Christian name from the United States.

LINNET—f Possibly derives from the Welsh Eluned, but more likely borrowed from the bird.

LIONEL—m Diminutive of Lionel given to the second son of Edward III, who was made Duke of Clarence.

LISE—f German short form of Elizabeth.

LIVIA—f The Roman family name.

LLEWELLYN—m 'Leader of men' (Welsh). Llwelyn, son of Iorwerth, Prince of All Wales, married a daughter of England's King John.

LLOYD—m 'Grey' (Welsh). David Lloyd George, British Prime Minister 1916-1922.

LOBELIA—f Modern plant name.

LOIS—f 'Famed in war' (Teutonic).

LOLA—f Spanish. Diminutive of Dolores.

LORA—f Another spelling of Laura.

LORETTA—f 'From Loreto' (Italian). A famous place of pilgrimage. Loretta Young, American actress.

LORNA—f Invented by R. D. Blackmore for the heroine of *Lorna Doone* in 1869.

LORRAINE—f French place-name.

LOUIS—m See under Lewis.

LOUISE, LOUISA—f Form of Louis. Supplanted in later days by Louisa but now the score is about even.

LOVEDAY—f Used in early times for a child born on a day when the family had made an agreeable settlement in business or family affairs.

LOVELL, LOWELL—m 'Wolf' (Anglo-Norman). A diminutive of the original Louve.

LUCAS—m Form of Luke.

LUCASTA—f Invented by Richard Lovelace, Cavalier poet, as the object of his verses.

LUCIA, LUCY—f Form of Lucius. Patron saint of those who suffer from 'distemper of the eyes', St. Lucy was killed in 303.

LUCIAN, LUCIEN—m Forms of Lucius. Lucian was second-century Greek satirist.

LUCILLA, LUCILLE—f Diminutive form of Lucius.

LUCINDA—f Romantic form of Lucy.

LUCIUS—m 'Light' (Latin). Lucius was pope 253-4. Lucius Apuleius, versatile Latin writer about A.D. 150.

LUCRETIA—f Roman family name. In legend Lucretia, raped by Sextus Tarquinius, killed herself.

LUCY—f As under Lucia.

LUDOVIC—m Latinised form of Louis.

LUKE—m 'Of Lucania' (Latin). Classic form of Lucas. St. Luke, author of the third gospel, patron saint of painters and physicians.

LULU—f Diminutive of Louise and Lucy.

LUTHER—m 'People's advocate' (Teutonic). Martin Luther (1483-1546), German religious reformer and translator of the Bible.

LYDIA—f 'Woman of Lydia' (Greek). Lydia Languish is the heroine of Sheridan's *The Rivals*.

LYN(NE)—f Form of the Welsh name Eiluned.

LYNDON—m 'From the lime-wood' (Old English).

LYNETTE—f 'Idolised' (Welsh). Medieval French form as written by Tennyson in his *Idylls of the King* (1872).

LYSANDER—m 'Champion of freedom' (Greek).

MABEL—f 'Lovable' (Latin). A short form of Amabel. Mab, Queen of the Fairies, is first mentioned in Shakespeare's *Romeo and Juliet*.

MABYN—f 'Youthful' (Welsh).

MADELEINE—f 'Woman of Magdala' (Hebrew). Mary Magdalene, a woman mentioned by St. Luke.

MADGE—f Short form of Margaret.

MADOC—m 'Lucky' (Welsh). Twelfth-century Welsh prince, subject of a poem by Southey. Ford Madox Ford—novelist of the 1920s.

MAGDA—f German short form of Magdalen or Madeleine.

MAGDALEN—f Form of Madeleine.

MAGGIE—f Short form of Margaret.

MAGNOLIA—f Flower name.

MAGNUS—m 'Great' (Latin). King Magnus I of Norway and Denmark, died 1047, was said to have been baptised Carolus Magnus in error after Charles the

Great (Charlemagne), the child's nurse thinking Magnus was a personal name.

MAHALAH—f 'Woman from Mahalah' (Hebrew). *Mehalah* by Sabine Baring-Gould (1880) reflects the use of this name in Essex at that time.

MAIRE—f Irish form of Mary.

MALACHI—m 'Messenger' (Hebrew). Translator of the Old Testament book named it from a passage saying, 'Behold I send Malachi'—which should have been translated as 'my messenger'!

MALCOLM—m 'Columba's disciple' (Gaelic). Very common in Scotland, after four kings ruling from 943 to 1165.

MALVINA—f 'Smooth-browed' (Gaelic). It appears that this name is wholly the invention of James Macpherson for his *Poems of Ossian* (1762).

MAMIE—f American diminutive of Mary.

MANFRED—m 'Man of peace' (Teutonic).

MANUEL—m A short form of Emmanuel.

MARCELLA—f Form of Marcellus.

MARCELLUS—m Diminutive of Marcus.

MARCIA—f Form of Marcus.

MARCUS—m 'Offspring of Mars' (Latin). Roman family name very recently revived.

MARGARET—f 'A pearl' (Persian). St. Margaret, beheaded in 275, is patron saint of expectant mothers. A daughter of Henry III was so called because her mother invoked the saint's aid in her labour. A very popular name with many forms developing. A royal name through the ages in nearly every country in Europe.

MARGERY, MARJORIE—f French pet-form of Margaret which has been a separate English name since the thirteenth century.

MARIA—f Latin form of Mary.

MARIAN, MARION—f A diminutive of Mary already common in the days of Robin Hood and Maid Marian.

MARIANNE—f French form of Marian or Miriam.

MARIGOLD—f Flower name of recent adoption.

MARISSA—f Uncommon diminutive of Mary.

MARIUS—m 'Of Mars' (Latin). Roman family name. Marius Goring (born 1912), actor.

MARJORIE—f Variant of Margery.

MARK—m Form of Marcus which has become much more popular. St. Mark, author of the second gospel.

MARLENE—f Short form of Mary Magdalene.

MARLOW—m Derives through an early surname from the place in Buckinghamshire.

MARMADUKE—m 'Servant of Maedoc' (Irish). An Anglo-Norman interpretation of the Irish, which has remained locally in the north of England.

MARTHA—f 'Noble lady' (Aramaic). The sister of Mary and Lazarus in the Bible. Canonised as the patron saint of housewives.

MARTIN—m 'Of Mars' (Latin). A pet-form of Marcus. St. Martin of Tours, soldier-bishop of the fourth century remembered in St. Martin's-in-the-Fields church.

MARY—f 'The longed-for-one' (Hebrew). The mother of Jesus, and so too holy to be much used in early days; but the very devotion of the common people brought it into common use.

MATILDA—f 'Strength in adversity' (Teutonic). Wife of William the Conqueror.

MATTHEW—m 'Gift of God' (Hebrew). St. Matthew, author of the first gospel. Captain Matthew Webb, first man to swim the English Channel (1875).

MATTHIAS—m Form of Matthew used to distinguish the disciple who took the place of Judas Iscariot.

MAUD(E)—f A form of Matilda introduced from France very early. Revived through Tennyson's 'Maud' (1855).

MAURA—f Irish form of Mary.

MAUREEN—f Irish diminutive of Mary taken up by Americans and revived in England.

MAURICE—m 'A Moor' (Latin). St. Maurice, third-century martyr.

MAVIS—f The old name for the song thrush, possibly introduced by Marie Corelli for a character in *The Sorrows of Satan*.

MAXIMILIAN—m 'Greatest' (Latin). The name said to have been invented by Emperor Frederic III, hoping that his son would combine the virtues of two great Romans —Q. Fabius Maximus and Scipio Aemilianus. So the name was used in German ruling families down to our own times. Used more often in its abbreviated form of Max.

MAXINE—f Popular French name which came to England via the USA.

MAY—f Short form of Margaret or Mary, but also standing for the month in which the child was born.

MAYNARD—m 'Strong and enduring' (Teutonic). Became a surname very early on. John Maynard Keynes (1883-1946), economist.

MEAVE—f 'The merry one' (Irish). The folk heroine later chronicled as queen of the Irish fairies.

MEDWIN—m 'True friend' (Teutonic).

MEGAN—f Welsh pet-form of Margaret.

MELANIE—f 'Black-haired' (Greek).

MELCHIOR—m 'King of Light' (Hebrew). One of the Three Wise Men.

MELINDA—f 'Sweet and soft' (Greek).

MELISSA—f 'A bee' (Greek). Legendary nymph who first taught the use of honey.

MELODY—f Used since the eighteenth century, but the reason for its first use is unknown.

MELVILLE—m Place-name—surname derivation.

MELVIN—m Place-name derivation but probably came from the USA.

MERCY—f An 'abstract quality' name arising in the seventeenth century.

MEREDITH—f 'Chief's name' (Old Welsh).

MERIEL—f Form of Muriel.

MERRELL—m Of Welsh or Irish derivation, indicating 'son of Muriel'.

MERYL—f Form of Muriel.

MICHAEL—m 'Close to the Lord' (Hebrew). One of the archangels, patron saint of the Crusaders.

MICHAELA—f Form of Michael.

MICHELLE—f French female form of Michael.

MILDRED—f 'Strength in meekness' (Old English). Victorian revival.

MILES—m 'Merciful' (Teutonic). The meaning can only be tentative, the name came over with the Normans and has been quoted as 'the crusher' or 'the warrior'.

MILLICENT, MELICENT—f 'Hard worker' (Teutonic).

MINA—f Short form of Wilhelmina.

MINNA—f 'Little lady' (Teutonic). Introduction into England influenced by Sir Walter Scott's Minna Troil in *The Pirate*.

MINNIE—f Pet-name for Mary now quite independent.

MIRABEL—f 'Wonderful' (Latin).

MIRANDA—f 'Deserving admiration' (Latin). Appears to have been invented by Shakespeare for the heroine of *The Tempest*.

MIRIAM—f 'The longed-for one' (Hebrew). A form of Mary. The name of the sister of Moses and Aaron.

MITCHELL—m A form of Michael derived from a variant surname.

MOIRA, MOYRA—f A form of Maire, the Irish Mary, which has gained ground in England in its own right.

MOLLY—f Pet-name for Mary.

MONA—f 'Dear Lady' (Irish). Name of an Irish saint which had a Victorian revival. Mona Lisa, famed portrait by Leonardo da Vinci.

MONICA—f 'Of good advice' (Latin). Origin uncertain. Saint who was mother of St. Augustine. Popular in 1920s.

MONTAGUE—m Norman family name from Mont Aigu near Caen.

MORA—f 'Sun' (Gaelic).

MORAG—f 'Great' (Gaelic).

MORDECAI—m 'Man of Marduk' (Babylonian). Used in the book of Esther.

MORGAN—m 'Man from the sea' (Welsh).

MORNA, MYRNA—f 'Beloved' (Greek).

MORRIS—m A variant of Maurice.

MORTIMER—m From the place Mortemer in Normandy.

MORTON—m From the English place-name.

MORVYTH—f 'Chieftainess' (Welsh).

MORWENNA—f 'Like a wave of the sea' (Welsh).

MOSES—m 'Drawn out of the water' (Egyptian), 'The great law-giver' (Hebrew). Its meaning can only be tentative. The great leader of the Jews.

MOSTYN—m 'Fortress' (Welsh).

MUNGO—m 'Lovable' (Gaelic). Mungo Park, eighteenth-century explorer of the Niger.

MURDOCH—m 'Man from the sea' (Gaelic). Rare now as a forename.

MURIEL—f 'Seabright' (Celtic). Another authority says it denoted 'myrrh'.

MURRAY—m 'Man of the sea' (Celtic). A well-known Scottish family name.

MUSIDORA—f 'Gift of the Muses' (Greek).

MYRA—f Said to have been invented by Fulke Greville (1554-1628) as the subject of his love poems.

MYRON—m 'Fragrant memory' (Greek).

MYRTLE—f One of the Victorian plant names which had such a vogue.

NADINE—f 'Hope' (Russian). A French form.

NANCY—f Diminutive of Anne.

NAOMI—f 'Pleasure' (Hebrew). The mother-in-law of Ruth.

NATALIE—f 'Christmas child' (Latin). French version of the original Latin, often used for girls born on Christmas Day.

NATASHA—f Russian version of Natalie.

NATHAN—m 'Gift' (Hebrew). More widely used in the USA. Hebrew prophet in the time of David.

NATHANIEL—**m** 'The gift of God' (Hebrew). One of Christ's disciples, better known as Bartholomew.

NEIL—**m** A form of Nigel.

NELLY—**f** Pet-form of Eleanor, Ellen or Helen.

NERISSA—**f** 'Sea-nymph' (Latin).

NESTA—**f** Post-Conquest Welsh form of Agnes.

NETTA—**f** Diminutive of Janet.

NEVILLE—**m** From the place Neuville in Normandy. Neville Chamberlain, Prime Minister 1937-1940.

NIALL—**m** Form of Nigel.

NICHOLAS—**m** 'Victor for the people' (Greek). St. Nicholas, fourth-century patron saint of children (as Santa Claus), sailors, pawnbrokers and thieves! Name of five popes, including Nicholas Brakespeare (as Adrian IV) the only Englishman so appointed.

NICOLA, NICOLETTE—**f** Italian and French forms of Nicholas.

NIGEL—**m** 'Little champion' (Irish). A Latinised version of Niall.

NINA—**f** Russian diminutive of Anne.

NINIAN—**m** Corrupted form of Vivian.

NITA—**f** Short form of the Spanish Juanita, which could be translated as Joanie.

NOAH—**m** 'Long-lived' (Hebrew). Noah built the ark and saved all species of animals from the Flood.

NOEL—**m** or **f** 'Christmas child' (Old French). For children born on Christmas Day.

NOLA—**f** Italian place name.

NORA(H)—**f** An Irish short form of Honora, now used independently.

NORBERT—**m** 'Famed in the North Land' (Teutonic).

NOREEN—**f** Irish diminutive of Nora.

NORMA—**f** 'Pattern' (Latin). Probably originates, in modern use, from Bellini's opera of that name, first performed 1851.

NORMAN—**m** 'Northman' (Old English).

NORRIS—**m** 'From the North' (French). A surname offshoot.

OBADIAH—**m** 'Serving God' (Hebrew). Hebrew prophet.

OCTAVIA—**f** 'Eighth child' (Latin). Could be used today for those born on the eighth day of the month.

ODETTE—**f** 'Fatherland' (Teutonic). In its French form. Odette Churchill was the British agent who survived Ravensbrück concentration camp in the Second World War.

OLGA—**f** 'Holy' (Norse). Much used in vintage spy stories.

OLIVE, OLIVIA—f 'Olive' (Latin). Olivia is a character in Shakespeare's *Twelfth Night*.

OLIVER—m 'Olive' (Latin). Oliver Cromwell (1599-1658), Lord Protector of the Realm. Oliver Goldsmith, author of *The Vicar of Wakefield* (1760).

OLWEN—f 'White clover' (Welsh). From an old legend, but spread in very modern times by the music *The Dream of Olwen*.

ONDINE—f 'Wave' (Latin).

OONAH—f A form of Una.

OPHELIA—f 'Succour' (Greek). Invented by Sannazaro in his *Arcadia* (1504) and perpetuated by Shakespeare in *Hamlet*.

ORLANDO—m Italian form of Roland. Orlando Gibbons (1583-1625), composer.

ORVILLE—m French place name. One of the Wright brothers, the first men to achieve powered flight.

OSBERT—m 'God-bright' (Old English). Osbert Sitwell (born 1892) one of a famous family of writers.

OSBORN—m 'God-like' (Old English).

OSCAR—m 'Spear of the gods' (Old English). Two kings of Sweden. Oscar Wilde (1856-1900), Irish writer of great wit.

OSMOND—m 'God's protection' (Old English).

OSWALD—m 'All powerful' (Old English). St. Oswald (605-42) was King of Northumbria and another saint of this name (died 992) was archbishop of York.

OSWIN—m 'God's friend' (Old English).

OTIS—m 'Keen of hearing' (Greek).

OTTO—m 'Rich' (Teutonic). Line of emperors of the Holy Roman Empire.

OWEN—m 'Young warrior' (Old Irish). A very popular Welsh name.

PALOMA—f 'Dove' (Spanish).

PAMELA—f Invented by Sir Philip Sidney for a character in his *Arcadia* (1590) and used by Richardson for his famous novel *Pamela* (1740).

PANSY—f Flower name.

PARKER—m 'Living near the wood'. English surname sometimes used as a forename.

PATIENCE—f Seventeenth-century 'abstract quality' name.

PATRICIA—f Form of Patrick. Made popular through royal choice for Princess Patricia of Connaught.

PATRICK—m 'Nobleman' (Latin). The name taken by the Celt, Sucat, when appointed missionary to Ireland (died c 468).

PAUL—m 'Small' (Latin). Saul took this name upon conversion to Christianity. The name of six popes.

PAULA—f Form of Paul.

PAULETTE—f A French form of Paula.

PAULINE—f A French form of Paula.

PEARL—f A modern gem-name.

PEGGY—f Pet-form of Margaret.

PENELOPE—f 'Weaver' (Greek). The faithful wife of Odysseus.

PENROSE—m English place-name.

PEONY—f Flower name.

PERCIVAL—m The great family name from Percheval in Normandy.

PERCY—m Short for Percival but used in its own right as a separate name from the great Norman family. Percy Bysshe Shelley (1792-1822), the poet.

PERDITA—f 'Lost' (Latin). A Shakespearian invention for the heroine of *A Winter's Tale*.

PEREGRINE—m 'Traveller' (Latin). *The Adventures of Peregrine Pickle* by Tobias Smollett (1751).

PETA—f A form of Peter.

PETAL—f Modern flower name.

PETER—m 'Rock' (Greek). One of the commonest forenames in every country. Given by Jesus to Simon, one of His three most favoured disciples.

PETRA—f Form of Peter.

PETRONELLA—f Diminutive form of Peter.

PETULA—f Origin uncertain. Petula Clark, vocalist.

PHILANDER—m 'Lover of his fellow man' (Greek).

PHILIP—m 'Lover of horses' (Greek). Philip of Macedon was father of Alexander the Great. One of the twelve apostles. Six kings of France and five of Spain.

PHILIPPA—f Form of Philip. Sometimes abbreviated to Pippa as in Browning's 'Pippa passes'.

PHILOMENA—f 'Nightingale' (Latin).

PHINEAS—m 'The negro' (Egyptian).

PHOEBE—f 'The shining one' (Greek). The Greek moon goddess.

PHYLLIS—f 'Leafy' (Greek). The subject of Greek and Roman pastoral poetry, a legendary girl who hanged herself for love and was changed into an almond tree.

PIA—f 'Devout' (Latin).

PIERS—m A French form of Peter but introduced so early that Langland wrote his 'Piers the Ploughman' in the fourteenth century.

PIPPA—f Short form of Philippa.

PLATO—m 'Broad' (Greek). Nickname of the great philosopher whose real name was Aristocles.

POLLY—f Diminutive of Mary.

POPPY—f English flower name.

PORTIA—f 'Porcine' (Latin). Unfortunate origin of a pleasant-sounding name used by Shakespeare for the principal female character in *The Merchant of Venice*.

PRESCOTT—m Old English surname derivation.

PRIMROSE—f Victorian flower name.

PRISCILLA—f 'Ancient' (Latin). From the Roman family name of Priscus.

PRUDENCE—f From the quality. Used as early as 348 for St. Prudentius, one of the earliest hymn-writers of the Christian church.

PRUNELLA—f 'Little plum' (Latin).

QUEENIE—f A name in its own right. Queen, as such, is not found.

QUENTIN—m 'Fifth' (Latin).

QUINCY—m French place name.

QUINN—m 'Wise counsel' (Irish).

RACHEL—f 'Ewe' (Hebrew). Younger sister of Leah as mentioned in Genesis.

RADEGUND—m 'Wise in battle' (Teutonic).

RADFORD—m Recent adaption of the surname.

RAE or RAY—f Short form of Rachel.

RALPH—m 'Wise counsel' (Old Norse). *Ralph Roister Doister* (c 1540) is earliest known English comedy.

RAMONO—f Form of the Spanish version of Raymond.

RANDAL—m 'Cunning fighter' (Old English).

RANDOLPH—m 'Wolf shield' (Teutonic).

RAOUL—m French form of Ralph of very recent use.

RAPHAEL—m 'Whom God has healed' (Hebrew). One of the seven archangels, the angel of healing. Raphael (1483-1520), Italian painter.

RAYMOND—m 'Wise protector' (Teutonic).

RAYNER—m Surname derivation today but originally the Teutonic 'folk counsel'.

REBECCA—f 'Heifer' (Hebrew). Wife of Isaac and sister of Laban. Becky Sharp is the central character in Thackeray's *Vanity Fair* (1848).

REDWALD—m 'Powerful adviser' (Teutonic).

REGINA—f 'Queen' (Latin).

REGINALD—m 'Enduring power' (Teutonic). Form of Reynold.

REMY—m 'Oarsman' (Latin).

RENATA—f Italian form of Reginald.

RENE—m 'Born again' (Latin). French version.

RENEE—f Form of René.

REUBEN—m 'Behold—a son' (Hebrew). One of the sons of Jacob, and the progenitor of a tribe of Israel.

REX—m 'King' (Latin). An innovation of the last hundred years. Rex Whistler (1905-1944), English artist.

REYNARD—m French form of Reynold. Reynard the Fox is a subject of Aesop's Fables.

REYNOLD—m 'Enduring power' (Teutonic). Gave rise to surnames from earliest times.

RHODA—f 'Rose' (Greek). First mentioned in Acts xii. 13.

RHONWEN—m 'Tall and slender' (Welsh).

RICHARD—m 'Tough ruler' (Old English). One of the most popular men's names throughout history with many diminutives and nicknames, like Dick, Dickie, Rick.

RICHMAL—f 'Sign of the leader' (Teutonic).

RITA—f Short form of Margaret originating in Italy.

ROBERT—m 'Shining fame' (Old English). A very popular name from the beginning of our language. Robert the Bruce, King of Scotland 1306-1329.

ROBERTA—f Form of Robert.

ROBIN—m A diminutive of Robert from earliest times, e.g. Robin Hood, Robin Goodfellow.

ROBINA—f Form of Robin.

ROCK—m 'Peter' in modern language.

RODERICK—m 'Far-famed ruler' (Teutonic). Last Gothic king of Spain (died c 711).

RODNEY—m 'Isle among the reeds' (Old English). Originally from Rodney Stoke, the village in Somerset which produced the surname. As a forename it benefited from Lord Rodney (1719-1792), the admiral.

ROGER—m 'Famous with the spear' (Teutonic).

ROLAND, ROWLAND—m 'Famous throughout the land' (Teutonic). One of Charlemagne's lords, subject of the *Chanson de Roland*, a medieval French romance.

ROLF—m 'Famed for his cunning' (Teutonic).

ROMOLA—f 'Woman of Rome' (Latin).

RONA—f Hebridean place-name.

RONALD—m Scottish form of Reynold.

RORY—m 'Red' (Gaelic).

ROSA—f 'Rose' (Latin). St. Rosa (1556-1617) has her feast-day on 31st August.

ROSALIE—f 'Rosalia' (Latin). Twelfth-century saint of Palermo noted for her extreme penitence.

ROSALIND—f 'Dragon rider' (Teutonic). Popular through the character in Shakespeare's *As You Like It*.

ROSAMUND—f 'Rose pure' (Latin). A fifth-century Hrosmund was compelled by her husband to drink his health in a goblet formed of her murdered father's skull! Rosamund Clifford, 'Fair Rosamund' and mistress of Henry II, died c 1176.

ROSCOE—m From the surname.

ROSE—f A flower name used from the very beginning of personal names, giving rise to a common surname and the old joke: 'Rose Rose sat on a pin—Rose Rose rose!'

ROSEMARY—f 'Sea dew' (Latin). A Victorian plant name.

ROSETTA—f Form of Rose. Town in North Africa where the Rosetta Stone was found (1799), which was the key to the deciphering of Egyptian hieroglyphics.

ROSS—m 'Fame' (Teutonic).

ROWENA—f 'Famed for friendship' (Teutonic). The Saxon heroine of Scott's *Ivanhoe* (1820).

ROWLAND—m See under Roland.

ROY—m 'Red' (Gaelic). But users of the name today usually have in mind the French *roi*—king.

RUBY—f One of the modern gem names.

RUDOLF, RUDOLPH—m Form of Rolf. Its popularity was increased by the fame of Rudolf Valentino (died 1926), heart-throb of early American films.

RUDYARD—m English place-name made famous by the poet Kipling.

RUFUS—m 'Red-haired' (Latin). William Rufus, King of England 1087-1100, was killed while hunting in the New Forest. The Rufus Stone marks the spot.

RUPERT—m Form of Robert. Introduced here by the popular Prince Rupprecht, nephew of Charles I.

RUSSELL—m 'Little red-haired one' (French). Developed from nickname to surname and thence to forename.

RUTH—f 'Beauty' (Hebrew). Meaning only tentative. Old Testament name.

SABIN(A)—f 'Of the Sabine race' (Latin).

SABRINA—f 'Severn' (Latin). The river.

SACHEVERELL—m An extinct family name. Sir Sacheverell Sitwell (born 1897), one of a famous writing family.

SADIE—f Diminutive of Sarah.

SALLY—f Pet-name for Sarah now used independently.

SALOME—f 'Peaceful' (Aramaic). A Greek rendering. She caused the death of John the Baptist as a reward for her dancing before King Herod.

SAMANTHA—f Origin unknown, but could be from Samandal, the undersea empire in the *Arabian Nights*.

SAM(P)SON—m 'Child of the sun' (Hebrew). Samson was the strong man of the Bible (Book of Judges).

SAMUEL—m 'He is of God' (Hebrew). Prophet following Moses and giving his name to books of the Old Testament which tell his story.

SANDRA—f Diminutive form of the Italian for Alexander, now quite separate.

SAPPHIRE—f Name of the precious stone.

SARAH—f 'Princess' (Hebrew).

SAUL—m 'The longed for' (Hebrew). The first king of Israel. Saul of Tarsus, when converted to Christianity, became St. Paul.

SAYER—m 'The people's champion' (Teutonic).

SCARLET—f From the colour.

SCHOLEM—m 'Peace' (Hebrew).

SCOTT—m A very early surname, obviously from Scotland. Used more in newer countries as a forename. F. Scott Fitzgerald (1896-1940), American novelist.

SEAN—m Irish form of John which is gaining popularity, perhaps after Sean Connery, actor in 'James Bond' films.

SEBASTIAN—m 'To be respected' (Greek). St. Sebastian was a Christian Roman soldier martyred by being shot through with arrows. Sebastian Cabot (died 1557), explorer.

SEBERT—m 'Fame in victory' (Teutonic).

SEFTON—m Place-name derivation.

SELENA, SELINA—f 'Heavenly body' (Greek). A moon goddess.

SELMA—f 'Fair' (Celtic). Derivation is tentative.

SELWYN—m 'Close friend' (Old English). Derives from the surname.

SERAPHINA—f 'Angelic' (Hebrew).

SERENA—f 'Calm' (Latin).

SETH—m 'Consolation' (Hebrew). More common now in the USA.

SEYMOUR—m From a French place-name.

SHAMUS—m Irish form of James.

SHANE—m English rendering of the Irish Sean.

SHARON—f 'The plain' (Hebrew).

SHEENA—f Gaelic form of Jane.

SHEILA—f The Irish form of Celia, but now quite separate.

SHELLEY—f From the surname.

SHERLOCK—m 'With hair cut short' (Old English).

SHIRLEY—f Place-name—surname derivation. Charlotte

Bronte's *Shirley* (1849) is believed to have set the fashion.

SHOLTO—m 'Saver' (Gaelic).

SIBYL—f 'Wise woman' (Greek). In classical times a mouthpiece of the oracle. Disraeli's novel *Sybil* (1845) may have led to its revival.

SIDNEY—m 'Of St. Denis' (French). Place-name in Anjou which identifies the great family of which Sir Philip Sidney was a member.

SIDONIE—f 'From Sidon' (Latin).

SIEGFRIED—m 'Victory and peace' (Teutonic). Hero of the German saga, the *Nibelungenlied*.

SIGMUND—m 'Shield of victory' (Teutonic).

SIGRID—f 'Beautiful as victory' (Teutonic).

SILAS—m 'Of the woods' (Latin). Short form of Silvanus, the Roman god of the forest. *Silas Marner* by George Eliot (1861).

SILVESTER—m 'Man from the woods' (Latin). St. Silvester is said to have cured the Emperor Constantine of leprosy. Spelled Sylvester it is also a line of popes down to the twelfth century.

SIMEON—m 'Listening' (Hebrew). Old Testament name which in the New Testament is always rendered as Simon. One of the twelve sons of Jacob. St. Simeon Stylites (died 459) spent the last thirty years of his life on a 60-foot high pillar.

SIMON—m New Testament form of Simeon, which may have the Greek element 'snub-nosed' implied in this later form. 'Simon, called Peter', one of the twelve apostles.

SIMONE—f Form of Simon.

SINCLAIR—m From the saint's name via the place-name.

SOLOMON—m 'Man of peace' (Hebrew). Solomon, King of Israel, noted for his wisdom.

SOMERSET—m Rare use of the name of the county.

SONIA—f A Russian version of 'Little Sophia', made popular by Stephen Mackenna's novel of that name (1917).

SOPHIA—f 'Wisdom' (Greek). Popular with German royal families in the eighteenth century.

SPENCER—m Short form of 'dispenser', housekeeper in a noble household. Charles Spencer, second Duke of Marlborough passed on his surname as a forename to Sir Winston Leonard Spencer Churchill. Spencer Perceval was the only British Prime Minister to be assassinated (1812).

STANFORD—m From the place-name via the surname.

STANLEY—m 'Stony field' (Teutonic). Place-name derivation. Made forever famous by Henry Morton Stanley's meeting with Livingstone in Africa in 1871.

STELLA—f 'Star' (Latin). Modern use attributed to its use in literature by Sir Philip Sidney, Waller and Swift.

STEPHANIE—f Form of Stephen.

STEPHEN—m 'Crown' (Greek). St. Stephen was the first Christian martyr. Five kings of Hungary and several popes have borne this name.

STUART, STEWART—m 'Steward' (Old English). Scottish royal family name which brought the Stuart dynasty to England with the accession of James VI of Scotland as James I of England.

SUSAN(NAH)—f 'Lily' (Hebrew). Wife of Joachim, the subject of *The History of Susanna,* one of the books of the Apocrypha.

SUZETTE—f Modern French diminutive of Susan.

SWITHIN, SWITHUN—m 'Strong' (Old English). St. Swithun (died 852) was Bishop of Winchester.

SYBIL—f Alternative spelling of Sibyl.

SYLVIA—f 'Wood nymph' (Latin). Sometimes Silvia. Rhea Silvia was mother, by Mars, of Romulus and Remus, founders of Rome.

TALBOT—m 'Woodcutter' (French). Based on the surname of the Earls of Shrewsbury.

TALIESIN—m 'Of the radiant force' (Welsh).

TAMAR—f 'Palm tree' (Hebrew).

TAMSIN—f A feminine form of Thomas.

TANCRED—m 'Thoughtful counsellor' (Teutonic). The King of Sicily who imprisoned Richard Coeur de Lion during the Third Crusade.

TANSY—f Plant name.

TANYA, TANIA—f An independent form of Tatiana, the Russian name.

TEDDY—m Form of Edward or Theodore used in its own right.

TERENCE—m Unknown meaning. A Roman family name (Terentius). Terence was a comic poet of second century B.C.

TERENTIA—f Form of Terence. Wife of Cicero.

TERESA, THERESA—f 'Reaper' (Greek). Really established in the western world through St. Teresa of Avila (1515-1582), and revived by the fame of St. Therese of Lisieux (1873-97).

TESSA—f Short form of Teresa.

THEA—f 'Goddess' (Latin).

THELMA—f Traced to the novel *Thelma, A Norwegian Princess* by Marie Corelli (1887) who, it seems, invented the name.

THEOBALD—m 'One of the bold' (Teutonic).

THEODORA—f Form of Theodore.

THEODORE—m 'God's gift' (Greek). St. Theodore, archbishop of Canterbury in the seventh century. Theodore Roosevelt, President of the USA 1901-09. In Wales takes the form of Tudor.

THEOPHILUS—m 'Beloved of God' (Greek).

THIRZA—f Possibly a Hebrew place-name originally. Shown as Tirza in the Book of Numbers.

THOMAS—m 'Twin' (Aramaic). One of the apostles (Doubting Thomas). Thomas a Becket (1118-1170), archbishop of Canterbury murdered in his cathedral.

THOMASIN(A)—f Diminutive form of Thomas.

THORA—f 'Of Thor' (Teutonic). God of thunder.

THURSTAN—m 'Like a thunderbolt' (Danish). Refers to the Norse god Thor.

THYRZA—f Relating to the Scandinavian god of war.

TIFFANY—f 'The manifestation of God' (Greek). A popular modern form of Theophania, perhaps after Tiffany's, the American jewellers.

TILLY—f Short form of Matilda.

TIMOTHY—m 'Honouring God' (Greek). St. Paul's companion.

TINA—f Pet form of Christine.

TITUS—m A Latin 'praenomen' of which the meaning is lost.

TOBIAS—m Form of Toby. Tobias Smollett (1721-1771), author of *Roderick Random* (1748).

TOBY—m 'God is good' (Hebrew). The Book of Tobit, whose son was Tobias, is part of the Apocrypha.

TOSTIG—m 'Sharp' (Welsh).

TRELAWNEY—m Place-name—surname origin.

TREVOR—m 'Home-loving' (Welsh). English version.

TRISTRAM—m 'Rumbustious' (Celtic). Mentioned in the tales of King Arthur. *Tristram Shandy* is a novel by Laurence Sterne (1767).

TRYPHENA—f 'Dainty' (Greek). Daughters of two of the Ptolemys of Egypt.

TUDOR—m See Theodore.

TURLOUGH—m A common Irish name of indeterminate origin but often translating Terence or Charles.

ULRIC—m 'Wise ruler' (Old English).

ULTIMA—f 'Last' (Latin).

ULYSSES—m The Latin rendering of the Greek Odysseus, hero of the legend. Ulysses S. Grant, general in the American Civil War, was President of the USA in 1868 and 1872.

UNA—f 'Lamb' (Irish).

UNDINE—f A water-sprite in Roman mythology.

URIAH—m 'God is light' (Hebrew). Husband of Bathsheba in the Bible. Any hope of its popularity was dashed by its use by Dickens for Uriah Heep in *David Copperfield*.

URSULA—f 'Little she-bear' (Latin). St. Ursula was an early martyr.

VALDA—f 'Powerful strength' (Teutonic).

VALENTINE—m or f 'Healthy' (Latin). A Roman Christian martyr of the third century who gave his name to the previously pagan festival of lovers on 14th February. One of Shakespeare's *Two Gentlemen of Verona*.

VALERIE—f 'Healthy' (Latin). From a Roman family name.

VALMA(I)—f 'May-flower' (Welsh).

VANESSA—f Invented by Jonathan Swift to represent Esther Vanhomrigh, the subject of his poems.

VASHTI—f 'Belt' (Persian).

VAUGHAN—m A recent borrowing of the old family name. Ralph Vaughan Williams (1872-1958), English composer, may have popularised the idea.

VENETIA—f 'Blessed' (Welsh). The Latinised form of the Welsh name Gwyneth. Venetia Stanley, renowned seventeenth-century beauty.

VERA—f 'Faith' (Russian). A recent introduction which may have been started by the character of this name in the very popular *A Cigarette-Maker's Romance* (1890) by F. Marion Crawford.

VERE—m 'Ver' in Normandy identified the great De Vere family who as Earls of Oxford had a great part in the affairs of England.

VERENA—f Swiss place-name, probably chosen simply for its pleasant sound.

VERITY—f An early 'abstract quality' name.

VERNA—f 'Born in the spring' (Latin).

VERNON—m A Norman place and family name.

VERONICA—f 'True remembrance' (Latin). The name applied to a cloth said to have covered Christ's face and which retained His image.

VESTA—f 'Goddess of fire' (Latin). Attended by the famous Vestal Virgins. Vesta Tilley was a music hall star.

VEVINA—f 'The sweet woman' (Gaelic).

VICTOR—m 'Conqueror' (Latin). Popular in England in the nineteenth century as a compliment to Queen Victoria.

VICTORIA—f 'Victory' (Latin). Queen Victoria, named after her German mother, set the fashion, which is slowly coming back again.

VINCENT—m 'Conquering' (Latin). St. Vincent, martyred in Spain in 304.

VIOLA—f 'Violet' (Latin). Heroine of Shakespeare's *Twelfth Night*.

VIOLET—f A Victorian flower.

VIRGINIA—f 'Flourishing' (Latin). A Roman family name but later and perhaps of greater significance a reference to Elizabeth, the Virgin Queen, after whom Virginia, the American settlement, was named in 1584.

VIVIAN—m 'Lively' (Latin).

VIVIEN, VIVIENNE—f Intended today as a form of Vivian though its true origin is lost.

WADE—m 'Ford-dweller' (Old English).

WALDO—m 'Stealer of power' (Old English). Waltheof, Earl of Northumbria, was executed by William the Conqueror in 1076.

WALLACE—m Scottish family name made popular by William Wallace (died 1305), who beat the English at the battle of Stirling Bridge (1297).

WALTER—m 'Popular ruler' (Teutonic). A favourite Norman name as shown in the great Fitzwalter family.

WANDA—f 'Of the family' (Teutonic). Ouida's *Wanda* (1883) may have started the fashion.

WARD—m 'Protection' (Teutonic). Element of many early names but deriving from the later common surname.

WARREN—m 'Warrior' (Teutonic). Warren Hastings (1732-1818), first Governor-General of India.

WAYNE—m Modern name of unknown origin used for its sound-appeal.

WENDY—f First written as a separate name by J. M. Barrie in *Peter Pan* (1904), inspired by a friend's little daughter who called him her 'friendy-wendy'. Also short for Gwendolen.

WESLEY—m Derived from the surname of the famous religious leader.

WILBUR—m 'Strong in defence' (Teutonic). Wilbur Wright and brother Orville made the first powered aeroplane flight in 1903.

WILFRED, WILFRID—m 'Will to peace' (Old English). St. Wilfrid (died 709), Bishop of York.

WILHELMINA—f Form of William. Queen of the Netherlands 1890-1948.

WILLA—f 'Helmet of resolve' (Teutonic).

WILLIAM—m 'Determination' (Teutonic). One of the most common male names since William the Conqueror and down the line of kings of England to William IV (died 1837).

WILLIS—m 'Son of William' (Early English).

WILMOT—m Pet-name for William.

WINIFRED—f 'Friend of peace' (Teutonic). Can also be the English form of the Latin rendering of the Welsh Gwenfrewi. St. Winifred was said to be a Welsh princess martyred by Caradoc.

WINONA—f 'First-born' (Santee).

WINSTON—m A place near Cirencester which identified a family and was then used in branches of that family as a forename and has since spread widely in popular use. There has been a Winston in the Churchill family since 1620.

WOODROW—m Surname derivation indicating 'a dweller by the wood' in Saxon days.

XANTHE—f 'Yellow' (Greek).

XAVIER—m St. Francis Xavier (1506-52), one of the founders of the Society of Jesus.

XENIA—f 'Hospitable' (Greek).

XIMENA—f In Spanish legend, the wife of El Cid, the great ballad hero.

YOLANDE—f An early variant of Viola.

YVES—m French form of Ivo.

YVETTE—f French diminutive of Yves.

YVONNE—f French diminutive form of Ivo.

ZACHARIAH, ZECHARIAH—m 'God's remembrance' (Hebrew). One of the prophetic books of the Old Testament.

ZADOC—m 'Just' (Hebrew).

ZEDEKIAH—m 'The Lord is righteous' (Hebrew). The last King of Judah and Jerusalem (597-586 B.C.).

ZENA—f 'Hospitable' (Persian).

ZENOBIA—f 'Living through the grace of Zeus' (Greek). Third-century queen of Palmyra who dared to oppose Rome and was defeated by Aurelian in 272. It has been used, unaccountably, in Cornwall.

ZILLAH—f 'Shade' (Hebrew). Once a popular gipsy name.

ZOE—f 'Life' (Greek). A rendering of the Hebrew for Eve which is comparatively recent in this country. Zoë was the Byzantine empress who died in 1050, having murdered her husband so that she could marry her lover!

ZULEIKA—f 'Brilliant beauty' (Persian). Favourite of Persian poets. *Zuleika Dobson* was a satirical novel by Max Beerbohm (1911).

Further reading

Barnhart, C. L. (ed.); *The New Century Cyclopaedia of Names,* 3 vols., 1954.

Partridge, Eric; *Name This Child,* 3rd edition, 1951.

Sleigh, Linwood and Johnson, Charles; *The Book of Girls' Names,* 1962; *The Book of Boys' Names,* 1962.

Withycombe, E. G.; *The Oxford Dictionary of English Christian Names,* 2nd edition, 1950.

Yonge, Charlotte M.; *History of Christian Names,* new edition, 1884.